A Very Virginia Christmas

STORIES
AND
TRADITIONS

Compiled and Edited by Wilford Kale

PARKE PRESS
Norfolk, Virginia

For my wife, Kelly

Christmas in The Trenches words and music © John McCutcheon
A Christmas Memory © 2006 Earl Hamner
Christmas on the Southside © 1995 Parke Rouse, Jr.

Book design by Marshall Rouse McClure

Published by
PARKE PRESS
Norfolk, Virginia • www.parkepress.com

in association with KHK Publishing, Williamsburg, Virginia

ISBN 978-0-9883969-0-6

Library of Congress Control Number is available upon request

Printed in the United States of America

STORIES

TRADITIONS

MISCELLANY

Introduction

I HAVE ALWAYS LOVED Christmas. Its spirit has been within me since my earliest childhood recollections. I remember waking up to a white Christmas at my grandparents' home and realizing what a special day it was when all kinds of traditions come together.

Later in my life, Christmas Eve, with its meaningful religious services, was added to the spirit. I remember being part of the service, holding a candle, and walking out of the church into an otherwise dark night singing "Silent Night."

I began to share my Christmas feelings with others when I became a newspaper reporter. I wrote my first Christmas stories for the Richmond Times-Dispatch in December 1974. Marjorie Webb Rowe, editor of the newspaper's newly developed Life-Styles section (formerly the women's section), encouraged me to write stories of Williamsburg and eastern Virginia, which my bureau covered. Often my stories received elaborate display space in the large Times-Dispatch Sunday paper on the Life-Styles section's front page.

Marg was especially grateful for any holiday stories that I could develop. The first was about Christmas in 18th-century Williamsburg, which I combined with what was on the holiday schedule of Colonial Williamsburg that year. Other stories included the English Yule log tradition, the first Virginia Christmas tree, and the traditions of numerous Christmas songs and carols. Holidays were festive and celebrated with great joy, so I tried, in my writing, to express those sentiments.

For more than a dozen years of writing for Marg and her successor, James Berry, I produced at least one Christmas or holiday story for their section. Those topics added variety to my other work as bureau chief.

My *Very Virginia Christmas* project began when I came across a monograph by Parke Rouse Jr., Williamsburg author and local historian. It was a short memoir of a Christmas he enjoyed in his childhood. In the 1920s, his family traveled by steamer across the James River from Newport News, Virginia, to visit his grandparents in rural Isle of Wight County, an area known as Southside. I told Marshall Rouse McClure, one of his twin daughters, that this great little story should be republished with others in a short Christmas volume. She had recently

republished a Civil War memoir, edited by her father, under the new title *After the Gunboats Landed*.

Then I thought about what other local Christmas stories might be appropriate as companion pieces in a small booklet. What about a larger volume about all kinds of Christmases around the country? Then, maybe a book just about Christmas in Virginia?

My enthusiasm heightened after I discovered a delightful Christmas story by noted Virginia author Earl Hamner.

Earl Hamner

Well-known for creating the long-running television series, "The Waltons," about his Virginia childhood during the Great Depression, Hamner has also written several wonderful novels, including *Spencer's Mountain*. After a lengthy telephone conversation with Hamner secured permission to republish his story, I knew we had the anchors for this book.

The project then took on a life of its own.

I began to research Christmas in Virginia. I have several dozen Christmas books in my personal library, and I went to them first. Later, as I began to research the wider resources at hand, I found there were a variety of stories, holiday traditions, and wonderful poems available.

Organizing the book in three sections has allowed me to include a wider diversity of "Stories" and "Traditions." The third and final section, "Miscellany," comprises some of my favorite holiday tales with no connection to Virginia. Because these "extra" stories help fill out the American Christmas narrative, I hope they will be welcomed by the reader.

Then, what about a title? Of all the possibilities considered, my publisher came up with *A Very Virginia Christmas* which seemed to say it all.

So, this is a collection of holiday bits and pieces, both old and new, that I wanted in my own book of Christmas stories and traditions. It contains something for everyone who loves Christmas and something for those who regard Christmas as "just another holiday." I hope, in the future, some of these stories may become part of your Christmas observance, whether you live in Virginia, New England, the Great Northwest, Mid-America, or along the Florida coast.

And I wish you always a very Merry Christmas and a Happy New Year!

Wilford Kale
Williamsburg, Virginia

STORIES

Today, I live far from the Blue Ridge Mountains of Virginia, but I still call them home, even though I work and live in the Hollywood Hills in Los Angeles, California.

How far I have come from those Depression days! In my Christmas Memory I tell of a night at the Baptist Church Christmas pageant when we children each received a rare gift — an orange!

Today from my study I look across the expanse of azure water of my very own swimming pool to where we have planted an ornamental orange tree. I pick an orange from time to time, and each time I do, I look back to that night during the Depression. They were years of great poverty, but in them we were richer than we knew.

A Christmas Memory

WHEN I WAS GROWING UP in Nelson County, Virginia, during the Great Depression, all the seasons seemed filled with a sense of wonder. I remember the dogwood spring, the watermelon summer, the russet and golden leaves of autumn, and frosty mornings that marked the waning year.

With the coming of fall, the pace of our lives quickened. The cry of the blue jay and the crow became more strident; a warning that winter was about to descend upon us. The world became alive with intense color as the leaves turned watermelon red, lemon yellow and pumpkin gold.

After the frost killed the vines in the vegetable garden, we gathered the last of the green tomatoes, and the following day my mother's kitchen would be filled with the pungent aroma of green tomato relish. Finally the long silent winter would flow down from the mountains, across the sleeping fields, the frozen lakes and ponds and into the woods and hollows where only the deer and the beaver, the squirrel and the rabbit were at large.

The first hint of Christmas came with the arrival of the mail order catalog from Sears and Roebuck. We called it "the wish book" and, while the great winter storms raged across the Blue Ridge, we would gaze wistfully at each page and dream our Christmas dreams.

Charlottesville was 24 miles away, and a walk down Main Street there during the Christmas season was as awesome as a journey through the streets of ancient Baghdad. Unlike the muddy country roads we knew, the city had paved streets with stoplights and streetcars and fancy window displays. We were foreign to all that sophistication and we showed it in our country clothes and country ways. We had little money to spend, but we did a lot of window-shopping with music at street corners provided by the Salvation Army playing a tinny version of "It Came Upon The Midnight Clear."

We had picked out our Christmas tree in July. We found it while picking blackberries up on Witt's Hill. It was a six-foot-tall cedar laden with cones and a pungent evergreen scent. A week before Christmas we brought it inside and set it up in a corner of the living room. We strung lights on it, and its fragrant presence permeated the house. It was as if we had captured some wild thing in the woods, brought it home and tamed it with tinsel and homemade icicles.

Ideally there was a snowstorm on Christmas Eve. If the flakes were small my Grandfather would predict the storm would continue for days. Sometimes it would diminish gradually at dusk, the moon would rise, and we from our window would witness a frozen cathedral of trees with crystal icicles clinging to the branches.

On Christmas Eve, bundled against the cold, we crunched our way down the snow-covered path to the Baptist Church. The steepled, white clapboard building beckoned with the warmth of a pot-bellied stove and the sounds of country voices celebrating the birth of Jesus.

The highlight of the evening was The Christmas Pageant.

Baptist Church in Schuyler, Virginia

Mothers had worked for weeks to improvise costumes for shepherds, wise men, and the Holy Family, others had rehearsed the actors who would portray Mary and Joseph. A manger had been set up, and a doll, the symbol of the Baby Jesus, rested in the crèche. Our Minister read the story with such power and drama that it was as if it were taking place right before our eyes:

"And there were in the same country shepherds abiding in the field, keeping watch over their flock by night."

As he read, three shepherds approached and, with the wise men, gathered together to admire the Baby Jesus. All the while the choir hummed "Silent Night, Holy Night." We were transported to Bethlehem. No more stirring drama was ever witnessed on the Great White Way itself.

When the service was over, Santa Claus arrived.

We knew he was really Mr. Willie Simpson who sang so loud in the choir. We recognized his voice from his "ho-ho-ho"s. From a burlap sack he distributed a single orange to each of the children.

We walked home through a frozen landscape, the sounds of our footsteps muted in the snow, the melodies of the old-time carols still resounding in our ears. The crystals of snow sifted down through the crusted overhead branches. In our hearts the spirit of Christmas had awakened. We did not feel the cold. We held oranges in our hands.

❅   ❅   ❅

EDITOR'S NOTE: In his novel, "The Homecoming," which became a television movie and precursor to "The Waltons" tele-vision series that ran for nine seasons in the 1970s, Earl Hamner wrote about how the Spencer family's father was late coming home on Christmas Eve. Clay-boy, the oldest child, went out looking for him while the others anxiously waited at home with their mother. The beginning and ending of this Christmas story add another flavor of a Virginia Christmas long ago.

Looking from her kitchen window, Olivia Spencer observed the ashen sky. It did not feel like Christmas. That moment which had always come in other years, that mingled feeling of excitement and promise, which she called The Christmas Spirit, had evaded her. Christmas had always been a time of rejuvenation to Olivia, a time to reaffirm her faith in God's goodness, to enjoy the closeness of friends and family; a time to believe in miracles again...

6

From the girls' room Becky called, "Good night, Luke," and Luke answered, "Good night, Becky; good night, Pattie-Cake." And Pattie-Cake called, "Good night, Luke; good night, Mama."

And Olivia answered, "Good night, Pattie-Cake; good night, Shirley." Other voices joined in a round song of good nights until all the people in the house has said so many good nights that they could not remember when they had said good night to and whom they had not. To keep the whole good-night chorus from starting all over again, Clay [Spencer] called, "Good night, everybody, and Merry Christmas!" and gave a long sleepy yawn, which was the signal that everyone had been bidden a proper good night. The house fell silent and they slept.

Around the house the world lay bright as day. The moon blazed down its cold light on an earth that was touched with magic. An ancient wind sighed along the ridges of crusted snow. Angels sang, and the stars danced in the sky.

Earl Hamner's boyhood home

Christmas on the Southside

THE WHITE RIVERBOAT rounds the bend of Pagan Creek, blows for a landing, and then slows as she approaches the dock. On the wharf, against a warehouse stored with Smithfield hams and peanuts, wharf hands stand by to catch the mooring lines.

With a great churning of creekwater, the S.S. *Smithfield* reverses her engines and slows her sidewise crawl toward the dock. Then, in a flash, mooring lines are thrown from ship to shore. From the dockside, friends and kinsmen peer alertly at the riverboat's passengers in search of city cousins coming to spend Christmas in the farms and villages south of the James River in Virginia.

A proud father on the steamer lifts his five-year-old for waiting relatives to admire.

"My, but he's grown!" an aunt shouts from the dock as the gangway is rolled into place and passengers begin to surge ashore.

Thus it began – the magic of Christmas in the country. In the simpler days when Woodrow Wilson sat in the White House, riverboats carried many holiday homecomers to the farms which lay along the East Coast's rivers, running inland from the Atlantic. In retrospect, they now seem splendidly romantic days, for bridges and automobiles would soon replace the white gothic river steamers and the horse-drawn vehicles which met them at the dock. Never since in America has life seemed quite so leisurely.

The arrival of the boat was Smithfield's chief weekday diversion in those days. Her "Here-I-come" toot at Red Point at 5:27 each afternoon was a signal to stevedores, farmers, and the idly curious to amble to the wharf and see just who and what came in that day from Norfolk or Newport News. The skipper, Captain Gordon Delk, was the idol of every child in town. He and his ship were little Smithfield's link with the glamorous world of department stores and movie houses which lay across the wide James River and Hampton Roads.

To the homecoming stranger, Smithfield offered a fragrant welcome. The whitewashed smokehouses along Pagan Creek exuded the hickory scent of a century of ham curings. The warehouses of Mr. Pembroke Decatur Gwaltney and Colonel Charles F. Day bulged with the fall peanut harvest from miles around. Richard Jordan's livery stable added its earthy ambience, while Shivers' Market displayed in the open air the day's offerings of oysters, rockfish, croakers, and catfish.

From Berry Hill farm my grandfather had sent Willie Bailey, a strapping farmhand, to load our luggage into the surrey and drive us to the farm. Strong arms were needed, for a horse sometimes bolted when it crossed the clattering wooden drawbridge at Wright's Point. Once or twice when a horse acted skittish, Willie dismounted and led it across.

December in southern Virginia is generally mild, though the sting of winter is usually felt during Christmas week. The last yellow leaves cling to maple and oak, while red berries on the holly warn that cold winds will soon scour the trees. Thick growths of mistletoe are exposed in the crotches of leafless trees, waiting for nimble boys to shinny up and collect them. Rows of cedar trees divide recently dug peanut fields, and pines look black against the pale winter sky. The gaudy profusion of summer is reduced to the cold geometry of fences and roads.

In the early 1920s, large flocks of migrating ducks still clustered in the blackwater creeks which drain from Southside Virginia into the James, flying up with a great roar of wings as we approached. Now and then a rabbit or fox would dart across the sandy road, startling the horses.

Then we reached Berry Hill. There in the yard stood Grandfather, calling out "Dismount! Dismount!" Grandmother was at his side, her thin white hair pulled upward and pinned in a knot. Close behind came uncles, aunts, a profusion of cousins, and the black farm boys, Willie Boy and Albert, who were dear friends and constant companions of my brothers and me. (It was years later before we knew my Grandfather had paid them to watch us and teach us to ride and hunt.) At first, Willie Boy and Albert could only stand and grin, but their embarrassment left them when the grownups turned us loose to play outside.

How many things there are to do in a week on the farm! We learned to eat persimmons ("No good 'til the first frost hits 'em"), to catch rabbits in a baited poke, to curry horses, to ride bareback and with a saddle, to find the eggs of renegade hens. We milked a cow, caught bull gudgeons in the creek, and did a thousand other things – some useful, some destructive.

If the weather turned cold, we sometimes helped with hog killing, though one bloody experience was usually enough. To make short work of it, all the men from the farm's half-dozen tenant families worked from sunrise to sunset to kill, scald, cut up, and salt the hogs, which had been raised the preceding summer. They were amazingly skillful, for Southside Virginians have perfected hog raising and curing since their fertile lands were first settled by Englishmen, a few years after Virginia was born in 1607.

Once the men had done their work, my grandmother directed the hired women in the making of sausage, cracklings, and the heavy gray soap, which they compounded of hog fat, lye, and other ingredients.

With the hams and shoulders of the hogs dressed, my  grandfather had them treated in the time-honored Smithfield fashion. First, they salted them in a large pot and covered them a day or so in brine. Then the hams and shoulders were cleaned, oiled, and hung in a draft. The procedure is similar to what the Roman writer, Cato the Elder, described in his *De Re Rustica*, written 249 years before the birth of Christ and discovered by Miss Bess Wright, a retired professor living in Smithfield.

"On the third day," old Cato wrote, "take them down, rub them with a mixture of oil and vinegar, and hang them in the meat-house. Neither moths nor worms will touch them."

After this treatment came the process of smoking the meat over a steady smoky fire in a curing house. This was accomplished with green hickory logs, which had been cut and stored outside the old brick smokehouse to await their hour of need. The hickory smoke smell of winter at Berry Hill will always remind me of Christmas.

While we youngsters were enjoying the outdoors, the ladies for several days prepared a memorable Christmas feast. In those days "getting ready for Christmas" primarily meant cooking, for prepared foods did not then exist. The big woodstove in the kitchen was kept busy from morning until night for days at a time. Fruitcakes and plum puddings must be made and aged in brandy. Smoked hams must be soaked and baked, black walnuts must be shelled for cakes, and hard sauce must be made of butter, powdered sugar, and brandy. The jobs were endless.

A holiday ritual, then as now, was the cheering cup before sitting down to dinner. Southerners called it a toddy and made it usually of corn whiskey or bourbon, water, and a teaspoonful of sugar. At Berry Hill, a Victorian shibboleth prevailed against women drinking. Therefore, my grandfather invited only the menfolk to gather in his room before dinner to quaff the welcome mixture before an open fire. A grandson had to be well along in college before being welcomed to the group.

Traditions in Christmas fare differ from house to house, but in southern Virginia in 1920 a Christmas dinner always included more food than any mortal could do justice to. At Berry Hill, a ham graced my grandfather's end of the table and a goose at my grandmother's. Between them ranged such heavenly temptations as creamed sweet potatoes, baked tomatoes, creamed onions, corn pudding, watermelon rind pickle, green tomato relish, homemade pickle, cornbread, hot rolls, and whatever else came to my grandmother's mind.

With so many to be fed at once, Christmas at Berry Hill filled the big dining room with tables and chairs. Though grandmothers in Calvinist households might make the youngsters wait for a second sitting (it was "good discipline"), my kindly grandmother would not hear of such inhumanity. She insisted that all the family sit down for one blessing, adults at one table and children at another. With Addie and Mary Polly in the kitchen, a relay constantly shuttled new provender to the tables.

As with any holiday feast, dessert was an important part of Christmas dinner at Berry Hill. Much advance work went into the mixing and baking of fruitcakes, which were soaked with brandy and placed with an apple to provide moisture while they aged for several weeks in the basement cool room. Another favorite was frozen custard made up of cream, milk, many eggs, sugar and vanilla. Frozen in a large ice cream freezer just before dinner, it was dished out and rushed on trays from freezer to table to prevent melting in the warm dining rooms.

Once, when the freezer broke, a farmhand valiantly transferred the mixture to a lard tin, half-submerged this in a washbucket of ice and brine, and vigorously turned it a half hour with his hands until it froze. Addie explained that this was the way poor people made their ice cream.

Southerners undeniably have a sweet tooth. New Orleans is famous for pralines and pecan pies and Charleston for Huguenot puddings and pastries. Virginia is no exception. In those days, before calorie-counting clouded our enjoyment of such sweets, our region seemed especially fond of grated sweet potato pudding or pie, made rich with butter and aromatic with bourbon and nutmeg. A showier dessert was tipsy cake or pudding, which had evolved from England's traditional tipsy squire and syllabub (meaning "silly stomach"). It is less common today, perhaps because few of today's cooks have the leisure to make sponge cake, blanch almonds, make brandy- or cherry-flavored custard, and whip the heavy cream which tops this heavenly mound. Such chores call for abundant "kitchen help."

The holiday week between Christmas and New Year's Day brought many other pleasures. Quail from one day's hunt turned up as next day's breakfast. Squirrels were boiled until tender and combined in Brunswick stew – a Brunswick County concoction of vegetables and meat stock with cured pork for seasoning.

The classic Berry Hill breakfast was lean slices of Smithfield shoulder fried in a skillet with scrambled eggs and served with eggbread. (Spoonbread and hominy grits usually accompany fried ham in the Deep South, but were not common in Virginia until recently.) Another smokehouse product was link sausage, called "dandoodles," which when aged became so strong and hard that they had to be parboiled before being split and fried.

Its ugliness was deceptive.

Berry Hill's kitchen was, fortunately, housed in a long wing of the house, an early American practice to prevent the spread of kitchen fires and the heat and odors of cooking. So the Berry Hill kitchen could safely indulge some of the family's taste for the malodorous and often maligned salted herring. Caught by Chesapeake Bay net fishermen each spring, these roe-bearing fish were cured in brine and smoked before making their way to the table in autumn. A night's soaking in water – sometimes with several changes – was necessary to desalt them for the skillet, where they sizzled and popped dangerously until ready to be borne into the dining room amid mixed cheers and protests.

The time-honored New Year's Day meal in some southern Virginia and North Carolina households is black-eyed peas and hog jowl, which Southern soothsayers say brings good luck in the months to come. This cherished dish was never evident at Berry Hill, nor was collard greens, which are often served with such "soul food." Instead, New Year's breakfast brought us goose hash and waffles or calves' brains and eggs. Whatever it might be, it was rich, delicious, and abundant.

In those days it seemed the right and proper way to enjoy Christmas. It was always with sadness that we bade Willie Boy and Albert farewell on the afternoon of New Year's Day. Then, as we waved good-bye to my grandparents while they stood smiling and beckoning from the porch – no doubt exhausted but still enthusiastic – we rode down the lane towards town and the waiting steamer.

Now, many, many years later, the smell of hickory smoke coming from an open hearth fire brings Christmas at Berry Hill vividly back to me. The dear faces, the riverboat, the surrey – now all long gone. But happy memories from childhood survive undimmed.

Plantation Christmas Days

IN VIRGINIA, where I was born, Christmas lasts not one day but a week, sometimes longer – at least, that is the way it was in the old slave days. Looking back to those days, when Christmas, for me, was a much more momentous event than it is now, it seems to me that there was a certain charm about that Virginia Christmas time, a peculiar fragrance in the atmosphere, a something which I cannot define, and which does not exist elsewhere in the same degree, where it has been my privilege to spend the Christmas season.

In the first place, more is made of the Christmas season in Virginia, or used to be, than in most other states. Furthermore, at the time to which I refer, people lived more in the country than they do now; and the country, rather than the city, is the place for one to get wholesome enjoyment out of the Christmas season. There is nothing in a crowded life that can approach the happiness and general good feeling which one may have in the country, especially when the snow is upon the ground, the trees are glittering with icicles, and the Christmas odors are in the air.

Christmas was the great event of the whole year to the slaves throughout the South, and in Virginia, during the days

17

of slavery, the colored people used to begin getting ready for Christmas weeks beforehand. It was the season when, in many cases, the slaves who had been hired out to other masters came home to visit their families. Perhaps the husband had been away from his wife for 12 months; he was permitted on Christmas to come home. Perhaps children had been hired out in another part of the state, or another part of the country, away from their mothers for 6 to 12 months; they were permitted to come home at Christmas.

It was made known during these holidays which slaves were to remain on the home plantation, which ones were to be hired out to the neighboring farmers, and which ones were to be sold. It was an important period to the slaves in many ways, but the feelings of joy at the reunion of the family prevailed above all others.

There were a number of festivities that led up to Christmas and prepared for it. One of them was the corn-shucking. No one who has not actually experienced an old-fashioned corn-shucking in Virginia can understand exactly what I mean. These corn-shucking bees, or whatever they may be called, took place during the last of November, or the first half of December. As I have said, they were a prelude to the festivities of the Christmas season. Usually they were held upon one of the larger and wealthier plantations in the neighborhood.

After all the corn had been gathered, thousands of bushels sometimes, it would be piled up in the shape of a mound, often to the height of 50 or 60 feet. Invitations would be sent around by the master himself to the neighboring planters, inviting their slaves on a certain night to attend the corn-shucking. In response to these invitations as many as one or two hundred men, women and children would come together.

When all were assembled around the pile of corn, some one individual, who had already gained a reputation as a leader in singing, would climb on top of the mound and begin at

18

once, in clear, loud tones, a solo – a song of the corn-shucking season – a kind of singing which, I am sorry to say, has very largely passed from memory and practice. After leading off in this way, in clear, distinct tones, the chorus at the base of the mound would join in, some hundred voices strong. The words, which were largely improvised, were very simple and suited to the occasion, and more often than not they had the flavor of the camp meeting rather than any more secular proceeding. Such singing I have never heard on any other occasion. There was something wild and weird about that music, such as will never again be heard in America.

While the singing was going on, hundreds of hands were busily engaged in shucking corn. The corn-shucking and the music would continue, perhaps, until ten o'clock at night. The music made the work light and pleasant. In a very short time, almost before any one realized it, hundreds of bushels of corn had been shucked. About that time a break would come. Everybody would be invited to a grove or some convenient place for supper, which was served in a sumptuous manner. After an hour, perhaps, spent around the table, the corn shucking, with more music, was begun again, and continued until late into the night, often into the early hours of the morning.

This was one of the incidents which usually preceded a Virginia Christmas time. There is another which I still vividly remember. It was at this season that the year's crop of hogs was killed, and the meat for the ensuing year was cured and stored away in the smokehouse. This came, as a rule, during the week before Christmas, and was, as I recollect, one of the annual diversions of plantation life. I recall the great blazing fire flaring up in the darkness of the night, and grown men and women moving about in the flickering shadows. I remember with what feelings of mingled horror and hungry anticipation I looked at the long rows of hogs hung on the fence-rail, preparatory to being cut up and salted away for the year. For days after this event every slave cabin was supplied with materials for a sumptuous feast.

Such simple and commonplace diversions as these broke the monotony of plantation life. Coming directly as they did before the Christmas holidays, they served to emphasize in the minds of the slaves the joyous season they ushered in.

Christmas itself, as I have said, meant a cessation of work for a week at least, and often as long as 10 days. Christmas Day the slaves would each receive something in the way of a present. The master who gave no present to his slaves was looked down upon by his fellow masters. He was considered unworthy to be classed among slave-holding aristocracy. The presents, in most cases, consisted of a new suit of clothes, or a new pair of shoes. I remember that the first pair of shoes I ever

 had the opportunity of wearing came to me in the shape of a Christmas present. Later on, when the war was going on between the North and South, we felt the pinch of hard times on our plantation. I received as a Christmas present a pair of wooden shoes – that is, the uppers were composed of leather, but the soles were composed of hickory wood.

In those days, the old people, as well as the young, used to hang up their stockings. The household slaves, and many who worked in the field as well, would hang their stockings in their master's or mistress's rooms. The children usually hung their stockings in the cabins of their parents.

It has been my pleasure and privilege to receive many Christmas presents, but I do not think I ever had a present that made me feel more happy than those I received during what was, as I remember, the last Christmas I spent in slavery. I awoke at four o'clock in the morning in my mother's cabin, and creeping over to the chimney, I found my stocking well-filled with pieces of red candy and nearly half a dozen ginger cakes. In addition to these were the little wooden shoes with the leather tops, which I mentioned.

The Christmas season ended with the cutting of the "Yule Log" for the next Christmas. My readers will know something of the "Yule Log," but will scarcely understand what the custom meant in the old days in the South, unless they have seen the "Yule Log" cut, and have counted the days that it burned.

On many of the plantations in Virginia it was the custom for the men to go out into the swamps on the last day of the Christmas season, select the biggest, toughest and greenest hardwood tree they could find, and cut it in shape to fit the fireplace in the master's room. Afterwards this log would be sunk into water, where it would remain the entire succeeding year. On the first day of the following Christmas, it would be taken out of the water; the slaves would go into the master's room before he got out of bed on Christmas morning, and with a song and other ceremonies, would place this log on the fireplace of the master, and would light it with fire.

It was understood that the holiday season would last until this log had been burned into two parts. Of course, the main point in the selection of the "Yule Log" was to get one that would be tough and unburnable, so that it would last as many days as possible. At the burning out of the log, there was usually another ceremony of song. This meant that Christmas was over.

As I look back in my memory to those Christmas days, thus spent as a slave-boy in Virginia, the present stiff and staid customs which prevail, especially in the larger cities, seem to me "flat, stale, and unprofitable."

Again I repeat, that in my opinion the real Christmas must be spent in the country, and I cannot but feel that there is in the Virginia Christmas atmosphere a fragrance and an influence which is not to be found elsewhere.

21

Based on the true Christmas story of the annual Holiday Train that brings Santa Claus to the poor towns of remote *Appalachia*.

Appalachia's Santa Claus Train

ESPITE WHAT YOUR PARENTS may have told you – there is a real Santa Claus. And I should know, because I've seen him myself!

Now before you think I'm absolutely nuts, let me tell you a little bit about myself. I was born in 1937 deep in the remote mountains of southwestern Virginia. Even as a very young boy, I remember how big and rocky those mountains were. Our tiny, two-room cabin clung to the mountainside like a crow perched on a tree limb. The soil was so hard and barren that nobody could make a decent living growing crops. If you ever saw where we lived, you might wonder why we didn't just get up and leave.

Daddy moved us there for two reasons – to be close to relatives and to work the coal mines. Daddy's family had worked in the mines for years, so when he was old enough, he grabbed a shovel and went to work. But even though we didn't have much, he provided everything we needed to live.

One day, Daddy was told he had to go off and fight for our country in some place I'd never heard of. After he left, my older brothers and sisters would read his letters aloud that he sent

23

back from these real exotic-sounding places. But one day, the letters stopped coming. Mama worried herself sick until the day some military men showed up on our doorstep. My daddy was killed in battle, they said, but rest assured – he had died bravely.

So Mama was faced with the hard job of raising my brothers and sisters and me alone. She could barely pay our bills, but there was really nowhere else we could go. We all slept in the same room, and there was barely enough food to make it through the day. When winter came, the bitterly cold winds would blow through the holes in the walls, and we'd huddle up against one another to keep warm. But we had many happy days – more than some families I know. I guess if you don't know what you're missing, then what you've got is good enough.

Like I said, where we grew up was very remote. There was only one winding dirt road, which led into the mining town, and it took so long to get there that we'd take combined trips with our neighbors to get supplies. Now when I say "town," I ain't talking New York City here. Our "town" had about three buildings: a bank, a barbershop, and a company store. But to me, going to town was an adventure, for it was my only contact with the outside world.

I remember Christmas being a very special time for us. All the families would decorate the local church and fix these huge dinners. We'd sing and laugh and have the biggest snowball fights you ever saw. And on Sunday, our own family would make a special trip to the cemetery to decorate Daddy's grave with Christmas flowers and ribbons. We figured he ought to celebrate with us, for Mama always said that he was still around, even though we couldn't see him.

As you may imagine, there wasn't much gift-giving going on. In fact, I really didn't know that people gave gifts during Christmas. That is, until I made a trip to town one day and saw a funny sight in the store window: a picture of a jolly old man in a red suit, jumping down a chimney with what looked like a bag full of presents.

"Who's that?" I asked Mama, pointing at the picture.

"Nothing, honey," she said, quickly turning me away. "It's just a picture."

Well, me being four years old at the time, that answer wasn't nearly good enough. Every time we'd pass that store, I'd tug Mama's sleeve and ask over and over again, "Who's that man?" And I began to notice that she was very reluctant to answer. In fact, it got to the point where we'd avoid the store altogether, and she'd send one of my older brothers in to get whatever we needed.

But one Christmas, I eventually wore her down. The mining town was filled with even more pictures of this mysterious old man, and I could barely contain my curiosity. So when I asked again, this was the answer my mama gave me: "His name's Santa Claus, dear. It's just a Christmas story some folks tell. He's not a real person."

I believed her at first, but then I started hearing other things at school. And when we'd go into town, I'd sneak a look at some of the Christmas magazines and books. I learned that, for someone who supposedly isn't real, an awful lot of people seemed to believe in him. He lived up in the North Pole and had a team of elves that built toys for him. And when Christmas came, he'd hop in his sleigh and deliver those toys to children who'd been good all year round. And we're not just talking down the street – he delivered presents as far away as China – all in one night!

I presented this evidence to my mother on Christmas Eve that year. And I told her that, other than the time I scared Mrs. Robinson's mule with a firecracker and the time I threw mud at Jimmy Harlan (he deserved it, by the way), I'd been a pretty good kid. Why hadn't Santa come out to see us?

My older brothers and sisters looked at each other with this sad look. And I remember tears suddenly filling my mama's eyes as she turned away. I wasn't too young to know that I'd just asked a question I shouldn't have.

You ever have one of those moments when you suddenly find out the truth about something, and everything around you seems to change? Well that's what happened to me that night. I looked around at our musty, cold cabin filled with broken furniture and empty cabinets. I noticed the old, ragged shirts we wore, their colors scrubbed out long ago in the hard stream water. I noticed the jagged mountains towering above us, blanketing us in dark shadows broken only by the candles we placed around the room.

I then knew the truth – Santa was real, and he wasn't coming to see us. Only children with real homes in fancy cities would find him sliding down their chimneys Christmas morning. Santa had forgotten us, and it looked like it was going to stay that way.

Talk about getting down in the mouth – that was me all over. I wasn't in the mood to do all the happy holiday stuff we did in years past. After all, if Christmas was a holiday for rich people, why should we bother celebrating it?

So as another year went by, I started dreading Christmas. The last thing I wanted to see were those red ribbons on the town lampposts, the wreaths on the church door – and certainly not that mean old man whose picture was hanging in the company store. Whenever everyone went into town, I'd stay at home and sit on the porch. I was six years old, and I already wanted to leave this place.

One day, I remember sitting alone on the porch throwing rocks at the fence post. Everyone else had gone into town, and a cold silence had filled the snowy valley. The distant whistle of the approaching 3:00 train suddenly filled the air, followed by the chug-chug-chug of the locomotive. It arrived every day like clockwork, and by its sound I knew my family would be home shortly.

It was then that I heard the frantic sound of footsteps running down the road toward our house. I turned and saw a sight that made my blood run cold – it was Jimmy Harlan, running breathlessly in my direction, his face red and his eyes wild. Jimmy was a very big boy with a mean streak to match. Obviously, I thought, he hasn't forgotten the mud-throwing incident from over a year ago. And now that my family was gone, he was going to take his revenge on me, the scrawniest kid in the valley.

"Wait!" he screamed as I bolted for the door. "I gotta tell you somethin'!"

As I slammed the door behind me, Jimmy ran up on the porch and looked through the window. Something in his eyes made me curious, so I asked, "What do you want?"

"He's here!" Jimmy yelled through the glass. "You gotta come see. Quick, before he leaves!"

"Who's here?"

"Santa Claus!" Jimmy gasped. "He's on the train!"

Now if Jimmy wanted revenge, he'd picked a good way to do it. I was already feeling lousy enough about Christmas, and now here was Jimmy rubbing it in. I had to give him credit – he was a pretty smart guy.

But to my surprise, Jimmy didn't wait for me to open the door so he could beat me to a pulp. Instead, he went running as fast as he could down the hillside, straight toward the approaching train. When he had gotten far enough away, I eased open the door and made my way slowly down the hill behind him – my curiosity had gotten the best of me.

As I got closer to the tracks, I could hear the sounds of people cheering. I ran faster and faster through the woods, the thundering train wheels growing louder and louder as I approached. I finally cleared the trees and found myself right up against the tracks. And what I saw next made my jaw drop.

A crowd of people had lined the tracks, waving and cheering to the train as it slowly inched its way past them. I wondered what the big deal was since this train arrived without fanfare almost every day – that is, until I saw the caboose. There, sitting in the back surrounded by big burlap sacks of gifts was Santa Claus – flowing white beard, big belly, red suit, and all, just like in the pictures!

"Ho! Ho! Ho!" he laughed heartily as he reached into the sacks and tossed toys, warm clothing and candy to the ecstatic boys and girls. "Merry Christmas! Ole Santa sees you." His team of elves surrounded him, and they didn't look like the tiny people I had seen in books. In fact, they almost looked like normal people – without the pointy ears, of course.

As Santa rolled on past me, he gave me a wink and threw a wrapped box in my direction, along with handfuls of hard candy. He then gave me one last wave and a hearty laugh before disappearing around the bend.

I remember standing by the tracks in a state of shock as Santa's train whistle faded into memory. To this day, I can't remember what the present was that Santa gave me, and it really doesn't matter. And year after year, Santa would return aboard "The Santa Claus Special," as it later became known. Word would spread like wildfire as the train approached, and the air was filled with what would become the traditional shout: "Santa's coming! Santa's coming!"

And as I grew older, I began to realize that Santa doesn't just live in the North Pole like all the books say. He lives in London, England, the African jungle and, yes, southwestern Virginia — anywhere that there are people who could use a little magic and joy this time of year.

How do I know this, you ask? Because almost 60 years later, I have become Santa Claus. When I looked old enough to play the part (the white hair and big belly helped), I slipped into the uniform, boarded "The Santa Claus Special," and returned to my mountain home. And although the area isn't as isolated as it used to be, the looks on the children's faces are still the same as mine was so long ago.

So yes, there is a Santa Claus after all. And you don't have to look very far to find him.

Santa Claus Special, circa 1983

George Washington: First in Christmas

OFTEN IDENTIFIED as "first in war, first in peace, first in the hearts of his countrymen," George Washington was the first real American trendsetter. As the first American president, Washington instinctively knew he was setting precedent with nearly every official act and with his own personal conduct as the first U.S. Chief Executive.

A brief look at some of his own history reveals that he could easily be labeled as "first in Christmas," too.

The native Virginian was renowned both before and after the Revolutionary War for his annual Christmas festivities at Mount Vernon featuring what is touted as his own unique recipe for holiday grog, possibly the first real American eggnog. To this day, this recipe is noted for its "kick."

The fact that Christmas was a disputed observance in America is clear from the very beginning. At Jamestown, Christmas was celebrated through adopted English customs. As the Virginia colony grew so did the holiday. Washington's famous Christmas parties were actually a family tradition, common amongst Virginia's elite of the 18th century. But some 500 miles to the north, at Plymouth Rock, Christmas was all but outlawed by the Puritan settlers – and it remained a subdued observance at best or ignored at worst during the pre-revolutionary period. The melting pot that would be called America was mirrored in its early attitudes about Christmas.

Two separate holiday seasons in the life of Washington reveal a great deal about Christmas in America in pre-revolutionary times and how others were thought of in context of the season. And a third Christmas to be remembered showed a lot about Washington's personal life.

The cold December of 1776, only months after the Declaration of Independence, Washington considered Christmas extensively in his plans for the Battle of Trenton. It would be a Christmas absent of décor, festive foods, and merriment. And it would be the Christmas that rallied Americans to the revolutionary cause.

Washington's Continental Army was on the ropes. In fact, as Christmas approached in 1776, morale was so low it was feared that the revolution was lost altogether. Washington's ongoing crusade was one of evasion and retreat – his forces continually fighting not only a better-organized enemy but also a lack of critical support and a wild American frontier.

In the dark moments of mid-December, a week before Christmas when the weather was brutally cold and the river waters dangerous to cross, Washington planned a daring attack for his 2,400 men who would cross the Delaware in the dead of night and march nine miles to attack a Hessian garrison.

The Hessian soldiers were no ordinary enemy. They were German mercenaries, allies of the British crown, sent to quell the American rebellion.

England's King George was serious in retaining control in the colonies, and he employed the most elite fighting forces in

George Washington at Valley Forge. Painting by Frederick Coffay Yohn

the world. Washington knew he could neither overpower nor go hand-to-hand with them. If he were to be successful, he would need, as he often did, to be crafty.

His was an audacious plan that Christmas. Washington figured he would catch the German troops unawares. They were known to celebrate Christmas, often with strong drink. His odds, Washington figured, improved with their Christmas spirit.

Though legend promotes the myth that the reason the Battle of Trenton was won by the Colonials was due to drink, modern research reveals this was not the case. The Germans were not drunk that night. But ultimately General Washington was right – they were celebrating Christmas and their guard was down.

In fact, the legend of the Christmas tree in America may have been born on this night as most modern historians credit those same Hessian soldiers with bringing the Christmas tree to these shores. As they gathered around their German-born traditional trees on Christmas Eve, Washington was marshaling his troops and their weapons onto boats and barges. As they gathered at river's edge, many ill-equipped for war and bad weather – some tying rags around their feet because they had no shoes – storm clouds gathered that first brought freezing rain, then sleet and then snow.

Washington was hoping to cross the Delaware and make the march in time for a pre-dawn surprise attack. But the weather was against him, slowing his progress. As the Christmas march towards Trenton made it to the New Jersey shore the army was added to by local colonists who joined in the march to support the fight, showing some Christmas spirit of their own.

The night and the day following turned out to be a Christmas never to be forgotten by both sides in the battle: Washington achieved the element of surprise, disrupting Christmas and winning the day over the Germans. Best of all, it cemented the sentiment that regular American citizens backed the revolution and enthusiastically supported the fight for freedom. It proved to be a bright early turning point in the unlikely success of the American Revolution that would drag on for many Christmases.

A prayerful George Washington in the snow. Engraving by John C. McRae

No Christmas of the Revolution, however, would be remembered more than the next Christmas spent by Washington and his troops at Valley Forge, Pennsylvania. Washington, after suffering several bitter defeats following the Trenton success, pulled his army into Valley Forge on December 19, just before Christmas 1777.

Surveying his situation, his heart was buried in regret and sorrow. His men were facing bitter cold temperatures while clad in thin clothes, many without shoes, housed only in tents. They were far from home, broke, and unsupported. As the snow fell and the temperatures dropped, Washington composed a letter of resignation to the president of the Continental Congress.

Outside his tent Washington heard a rustle. Was it the sound of mutiny? One of his officers earlier had predicted such.

Without donning his coat he walked out into the cold to investigate, looking upon men huddled around fires as he walked. They were cooking whatever game they could find, thrown into pots to boil over the fires, filling the air with a variety of strange aromas.

But in the spirit of Christmas, men in these desperate circumstances still cheered Washington: "Long live the United States! Hail to our Chief! May Liberty prevail!"

As Washington braved the cold and walked among his troops from group to group and tent to tent, he asked his men if they had not suffered enough. "Having come this far," one lieutenant said, "we can but go the rest of the distance."

As he returned to his own tent, Washington and an aide were stunned to see that in his absence from his quarters some men had draped garlands of holly and cedar above the tent-flap door.

General Washington took the letter he had started to Congress. He burned it at the fire his aides had built outside his tent. "May God relieve your sufferings, if the Congress will not.

And a good Christmas to you!" he said.

The famed portrait of Washington kneeling in prayer at Valley Forge is much easier to envision with this Christmas celebration as a backdrop.

Unknowingly, Washington began a tradition of military Christmas during his service in the American Revolution – a tradition that has inspired, no doubt, thousands of common foot soldiers in the fight for freedom ever since.

But there was one more historic Washington Christmas event – this one even more personal.

The warfare of the American Revolution had concluded, and the treaty to formally end the war was being negotiated. Sometime in the fall of 1783, Washington apparently promised his wife, Martha, that he would return to her by Christmas.

By November, Washington was taking possession of the last British stronghold – New York City – and later in the month received word that the treaty had been signed. But before he could return to Virginia, Washington needed to bid farewell to his troops and resign his commission as commander and then make his way to Mount Vernon.

For him, everything began to fall into place.

One of Washington's most memorable speeches was his farewell to his officers on December 4 at Fraunces Tavern in New York. "With a heart full of love and gratitude I now take leave of you," he said.

Washington and his entourage were then taken to Whitehall wharf, where they embarked on a barge for Paulus Hook, New Jersey, and his journey home. It took days, however, by horse, carriage, and boat, working their way through New Jersey to Philadelphia. There he was greeted with illuminations and parades, but managed to buy some Christmas gifts for Martha and her two grandchildren, Eleanor Parke and George Washington Parke Custis, whom they had adopted. Then via

Wilmington, Delaware, he arrived in Annapolis, Maryland, where the Continental Congress was meeting.

The weather was mild, but the journey was still tiring. The end of his work, as he felt then, was in sight. On December 23, he delivered his farewell address to the Congress and submitted his resignation as commander-in-chief. He left Annapolis quickly because time was fleeting.

After an overnight in Bladensburg, Maryland, he rode to the Potomac River and crossed by ferry to Alexandria, Virginia and rode by horseback the final miles to Mount Vernon, arriving after dark on Christmas Eve.

What a homecoming it must have been and what a Christmas awaited him as he returned, after eight long years, to be with his family. It had to be a Christmas where the phrase "peace on earth and good will to all men" stirred Washington's heart.

As we now look at Christmas it is probably fitting that a heavy snowstorm struck Mount Vernon on the next day, Christmas morn, with all the surrounding countryside covered in snowdrifts. Thus allowing Washington to celebrate with just his family.

George Washington's Virginia home, Mount Vernon

A Christmas in the 1960s

WHEN I WAS YOUNG and the world was new, at that wonderful age of six, my younger brother and I celebrated our first Christmas in the Shenandoah Valley of Virginia at the family homeplace where my Dad was born and raised. Called "Chapel Hill" (all these old Southern homes have names), the gracious Georgian-style house has been in the family since 1816. In those early days, brother John and I had only just grasped the concept of Santa Claus because our family had spent the previous three years in Taiwan where my parents taught English and only returned to the States that previous summer.

Everything about an American Christmas was new and wondrous to us, especially the amazingly generous fat guy in the red suit who was just waiting to give us presents. But it seemed that he required snow, the cold white stuff we had not yet witnessed, for sleigh travel with his flying deer. A bit eccentric perhaps, but I was an imaginative child and willing to indulge him. It wasn't lost on us, though, that this weather phenomenon didn't fall from a clear blue sky.

Our parents hadn't made much of Christmas in Taiwan. We

were tiny tots and toys scarce, the few there were being some that other missionary families shared with us from those their children had outgrown. There were no toy stores in Taiwan then like there were here. Chewing gum was a major treat. We caught our breath at the delights we saw in the American shops.

"Barbie" dolls had just been introduced and I longed for one with hair to comb, an endless perfect wardrobe, and furniture of her own. John had his eye on a racing car set. We'd seen picture books with Santa in them and there was always snow. What to do, what to do? Nothing but wait and hope.

The journey to Virginia began in the mountains of Tennessee, jolting along in our old Ford on Route 11 to Augusta County in the Shenandoah Valley. Our grandmother, whom we all called Mommom, Aunt Moggie, Uncle RW, and our five cousins awaited us on the family farm.

Dad spent what seemed like days in preparation for the trip, packing and repacking the car. Finally we got underway. I'm amazed as an adult to find that the trip normally takes about six hours, or less, because I have vivid memories of this ride going on all day and far into the night, playing "I Spy with My Little Eye," and singing carols until we were hoarse and my parents must've been nearly half mad.

Mom taught us a song on the way about Santa, "You'd Better Watch Out," a worrisome ditty. I wasn't an exceptionally naughty child, but knew there were the occasional times when I had been what, in some person's minds, might be construed as bad. What if Santa, this wonderful provider, had seen me at less than my best? What if I got switches?

My father told us about his Uncle Gus who'd received switches. Horrors of horrors. Deep down I felt it was no more than I deserved if my every move had been carefully noted. I hoped Santa was a forbearing fellow, but doubts lurked, a new worry on top of the snow thing.

The Churchman family home, "Chapel Hill"

Eventually we arrived in the Valley and the paved highway turned into bumpy dirt roads as we wound deeper into the country with its unique smells. My father pointed out the lights of Chapel Hill glowing in the distance, then unbelievably we were driving up the long lane, and the yard filled with family to warmly welcome the weary travelers.

The first night we went straight to bed. I slept upstairs in the yellow room – every room has a name – with my two cousins, Margaret and Elizabeth Page. In the morning, John and I got our wish. We awoke to heavily falling snow, a magical time. We went sledding down the lane, made a giant snow bunny with my father and had the time of our lives, clambering back into the kitchen ravenous and soaking wet. We peeled off layers of pants – no snow pants back then – and took our wet clothes and mittens to hang them by the stove in Mommom's room, before downing bowls of homemade soup.

The day before Christmas finally came, the old brick house was filled with tantalizing smells. The kitchen door opened periodically, the sleigh bells on it announcing the arrival of yet more friends bringing yet more gifts. Friends, neighbors, and family all exchanged gifts, even if it was only a plate of cookies exchanged for yours.

Presents were stashed in every corner of the front room, covering the old piano and stacked beneath, wrapped in paper and ribbons which I found almost too beautiful to bear. I knew there were some for me among them, that I was not in total reliance on Santa. Even so, I longed to be kindly remembered by him.

As any child can attest, Christmas Eve is the longest day of the year and one in which we made extreme nuisances of ourselves, asking endless questions and climbing over and under the furniture to see which gifts were ours. At last we gathered together in the front room in the presence of the magnificent pine decorated shortly before our arrival. My uncle cut it from a nearby woods, and I loved its fresh smell, also new to me. A stern glance from him quieted us down and my grandmother read the Christmas story from *The Book of Matthew*.

The ancient story evoked a newfound sense of awe at the holiness of this night as I gazed at the little wooden creche and the figures carved by my father. I felt the love in the room and understood that it had something to do with this sacred child whose birth we were celebrating.

All right, Jesus loved me, so did God, but what about Santa? After all, he was the one to fill the stocking I'd hung carefully in between my cousins' on the mantel under the portrait of our great-great grandmother. All of our stockings had been knitted for us by our elderly relative and had a scene of Santa on one side and a reindeer on the other with little bells that jingled when I lifted it. A reminder of his imminent arrival.

After the stockings were hung and *The Night Before Christmas* read, we heard sleigh bells ringing far off in the meadow. Good heavens, Santa was that close. We tumbled over each other in our haste to get to bed lest the old guy should discover us still up and promptly leave. Touchy fellow, peculiar ways, but ours was not to question why. We scampered under the covers and did not dare to peep until dawn.

After that, it was every child for him or herself. We launched out of bed, vying to be the first one to wish each other "Christmas Gift!" We then paced about in acute impatience while the adults had a leisurely breakfast – Who could eat at a time like this? – and dressed with slow, careful deliberation. I was wearing the same clothes I'd donned two days ago. As for bathing, only under duress.

We practically gave up all hope of ever seeing inside the front room and paced outside the closed double doors where no child could enter until everyone had gathered. Mommom, her blue eyes twinkling, reported that Santa had come and relieved our troubled minds. Uncle RW told us he'd seen reindeer hoof prints in the snow on the roof of the house. Imagine that. We never once questioned what he'd been doing on the roof. Not that this would make the slightest difference if we eked out our days waiting in the hall.

Then, glory hallelujah, the family assembled and lined up according to age, as required by the law of our clan. The all-important doors opened. Great was our wonder. There was the tree lit, the stash of presents sorted into individual piles, and the stockings filled. Mine bulged with promise. Praise be! The old fellow was extremely tolerant. I'd truly feared to see those switches.

It's ages later now, and Mommom has gone on before us. Lining up outside those omnipotent doors with my brother, cousins, parents, aunt, uncle, and her at the end is a distant cherished memory. Christmas is a place I return to in my thoughts whenever I need the sense of joy and reassurance it brings. And I remember that time so long ago when my brother and I despaired of snow.

A Coniurer. Their Idoll A Preist

Their Coniuration about
C: Smith 1607

DENNIS MONTGOMERY

Captain John Smith's Christmas

THE EVER-SCRIBBLING Captain John Smith wrote the first report of a Christmas celebration in English North America. In a sentence often reprinted, he detailed a Yuletide feast of shell food and meat and poultry and other jolly goodies devoured in the snug huts of a hospitable band of Indians beside the Chesapeake Bay.

His account occasionally is mistaken for the relation of the continent's original English Christmas, but Smith's anecdote is no more than the first description of one in the First Colony. There is a difference between the first time a thing happened and the first time that thing was written about.

In any case, the captain detailed neither the first December 25 he passed in the brand-new Old Dominion, nor the first that Anglo-Saxons abided on these shores, nor the first that Europeans spent in the Western Hemisphere. Nor was it on what we call Christmas.

Nevertheless, Smith's sentence is worth reprinting once more. It is part of a narrative that begins at Jamestown on December 29, 1608 – by the Old Style calendar the 17th-century English used. As they often were in winter, the settlement's

45

inmates were famished, and, not for the first time, Smith was off on the hunt of provender. With a barge, a boat, and 46 men, he set off down the James River. He planned to round Old Point Comfort, where Virginia's Lower Peninsula pokes into the bay, make his way up the York, and land at the north-bank Indian village Werowocomoco to barter with Powhatan, headman of a loose association of Tidewater tribes, for a boatload of corn. Powhatan asked to be paid with construction of an English-style house, a grindstone, 50 metal swords, firearms, a cock, a hen, and, for good measure, copper and beads.

The captain and his company, who would have sailed downstream with the outgoing tide, made about 22 miles the first day. They spent the night at Warraskoyack, an aboriginal enclave up Pagan Creek on the James's south side near modern Smithfield. It sounds as if in the morning a winter nor'easter – the direction Smith was going – was starting to blow. But, with 12 of his bunch, he left for Kecoughtan, a village of natives about six miles across Hampton Roads, at the confluence of the James and today's Hampton River – modern Hampton. Now the ingeminate sentence:

> The next night being lodged at Kecoughtan; six or seaven
> dayes the extreame winde, rayne, frost and snow caused us
> to keep Christmas among the Salvages, where we were never
> more merry, nor fed on more plentie of good Oysters, Fish,
> Flesh, Wild-foule, and good bread; nor never had better fires
> in England, then in the dry smoaky houses of Kecoughtan.

The description originally appeared in Smith's travel tale *The Proceedings of the English Colonie in Virginia since the first beginning from England in the yeare of our Lord 1606, till this present 1612, with all their accidents that befell them in their Journies and Discoveries*. That 110-page tome was the third of more than a dozen of Smith's literary endeavors that fell from the press. Twelve years later, he recycled the passage in his eighth, the six-part, 248-page *The Generall Historie of Virginia, New-England, and the Summer Isles with the names of the Adventurers, Planters and Government from their first beginning in 1584 to this present 1624.*

The Werowocomoco expedition began four days after the anniversary of the Nativity. Smith spent December 25 at Jamestown. How is it, then, the captain said he kept Christmas at Kecoughtan? He didn't land there until December 31.

It is tempting to think that he meant to say he was celebrating New Year's Eve, but, by the Old Style calendar, New Year's Eve was March 24. However, in Smith's day, by custom, Christmas began December 25 and lasted through Twelfth Night, or January 6.

We've found no account of the colonists' 1607 Christmas, their first in Virginia, nor of their 1606 observances on the outbound voyage, their first as Virginia settlers.

By Christmas 1607, all but 38 of 105 settlers were dead or gone – felled by Indians, disease, sloth, starvation, cold, and melancholy. A couple had skedaddled back to England.

The Reverend Mr. Robert Hunt lasted a month or so longer. Smith called him "our honest, religious and courageous divine." Conscientious in his performance of the Church of England's rituals, it is doubtful Hunt neglected services on Christ's birthday. We don't know.

The captain wrote no account of that Yule's celebrations; but he was absent, off foraging then, too, on a ramble that appears to have put him in a tight spot.

About December 10, 1607, Smith took a squad of men up the James and into the tributary Chickahominy River scrounging for victuals, and within two days was snared by a hunting party which Powhatan's kinsman Opechancanough commanded. The Indians killed a handful of the party, some survivors fled

for Jamestown, and Smith went walkabout with his captors. The trek took him north to, by best guess, the Rappahannock, the river next above the York, on Christmas Day. In his descriptions of his travels from Indian camp to Indian camp, Smith mentions Christmas not at all, which, under the circumstances, is not hard to understand.

Kecoughtan Indian, from the John Smith map of 1612

They came at length to Werowocomoco, where Opechancanough introduced Smith to Powhatan. On January 1, 1608, Powhatan sent Smith back to Jamestown with much-needed supplies.

It should be said 1607 was not the year of the first English Christmas in North America. Not by 23. Smith's *Generall Historie*, says the English colonies had "their first beginning in 1584."

Englishmen and Englishwomen first passed a New World Yuletide during the 16th-century attempt to settle Roanoke Island. Sir Walter Ralegh, the sponsor, dispatched exploratory voyages in 1584, and 108 settlers in 1585.

Roanoke Island is within the Outer Banks of today's North Carolina. Ralegh christened his holdings "Virginia," in honor of his benefactress, the virgin Queen Elizabeth I.

The Roanoke Islanders endured hardship, adventure, and privation for more than a year before catching a ride home with the passing Sir Francis Drake, headed back to England fresh from a raid on the Spanish at Cartagena. During their stay, a party of Roanoke explorers ventured northward into modern Hampton

Roads, seem to have spent the winter, and may have become the first English to enjoy Christmas in modern Virginia proper.

EDITOR'S NOTE: There are no references to any Christmas festivities either at Roanoke in the 1580s or at early Jamestown. Ironically, the settlement voyage, which landed at Jamestown in May 1607, began in England on December 20, just a few days prior to Christmas. No records or recollections of that voyage mention any events on Christmas Day, even though the three ships were still within English waters.

One of the passengers was the Rev. Robert Hunt, who probably had a prayer service on Christmas day, but it was not mentioned in any surviving accounts of that voyage.

After Captain Smith returned to England in 1609, there was no mention of Christmas at Jamestown for many, many years.

References to Christmas began to appear in the *Virginia Statutes at Large* established by the House of Burgesses meeting annually at Jamestown. The Christmas season served as a calendar benchmark for various laws. For example in October, 1629 the Burgesses decided that the colony should attack the Indians at various times each year. The Pamunkey Indians were targeted for attack "before the frost of Christmas."

In 1631, legislation was adopted requiring that churches be constructed in areas where there are none, or where buildings were in disrepair. Such action was to take place before the "feast of the nativitie of our Saviour Christ."

In 1642 an act was adopted requiring ministers and churchwardens to meet before local commanders in the county court "every year, after Christmas."

Although Christmas was a religious and social focal point, there is very little in existing records to show how the holiday was celebrated in Virginia throughout the 17th century.

JULIE ANN GOCHENOUR

A Shenandoah Valley Christmas

YEARS AGO in the Shenandoah Valley, the time from Thanksgiving to Christmas slowed to the speed of frozen molasses. For children the weeks were thick, sweet, and clogged with expectation: a heady mix of dreams, wishes, secrets, and anticipation. For adults, the rushed pace of autumn's crop and apple harvests gave way to hunting season, hog butchering, and the onset of winter chores and tasks.

The coming Christmas season, for young and old alike, embraced a sequence of preparations and traditions that began with black walnuts and ended with the aroma of baked spices, the scent of fresh pine and cedar, and the smell of warm dry livestock bedded down on clean straw in the stables, stalls, and pens located under every bank barn.

But a rural Shenandoah Valley Christmas always started with black walnuts. The rich, pungent nutmeats were a staple ingredient in holiday cakes, cookies, candies, and even pies. Every fall parents sent the children out to gather bushels of walnuts in gunny-sacks and buckets, the green, split, weeping hulls staining hands and fingers brown for weeks to come. One way or another, families shucked the walnuts and, when the

51

hard, black, ridged, wrinkled meats were freed from their hulls, they were dumped on the barn or shed floor to dry and cure. Butternuts and hickory nuts might follow, but with the black walnuts gathered, some form of Christmas treat was sure.

Soon after, hunting season got underway. No one spoke of Christmas yet, but thoughts of the holiday were beginning to stir and seep into daily activities. Family members hunting the fields with a rifle or shotgun for rabbit, squirrel, deer, or turkey began noticing the shape, color, and height of potential Christmas trees. Hauling firewood and logs out of the mountain, the men passed the prettiest stands of mountain laurel, densest patches of now-endangered running cedar. And while Christmas was still weeks away, everyone began eyeing the thickest strands of orange bittersweet twining around rundown fencerows, the heaviest branches of hemlocks and red spice berries hanging over the creeks and spring branches.

November brought hunting season, Thanksgiving, and butchering day to rural families in quick succession. Hog butchering provided rural families with meat and started as soon as temperatures dropped enough that fresh pork could safely be stored and cured in the meat house without fear of spoiling. Once the sausage and scrapple was made; the lard and cracklings rendered; the hams, shoulders, and sides of bacon patted down with salt, pepper, and brown sugar to cure; the sausage, tenderloin, backbone, and spareribs packed and canned in clear quart and half-gallon Mason jars; a delightful welter of Christmas preparations could begin.

Christmas baking was always first. Shenandoah Valley housewives made their shopping lists carefully, calculating the amount of salt, sugar, molasses, raisins, spices, and cocoa they would need for applesauce cakes, ginger cookies, snicker doodles, brown sugar drops, raisin jumbles, and dozens upon dozens of sugar cookies as well as fudge, fondant, divinity, and candied nuts such as penuche. There were also specialty items purchased just once a year specifically for the Christmas season. These varied according to each family's particular tastes and traditions but might include baking ammonia needed to make the obligatory lemon crackers; candied fruits, brazil nuts and the like for fruit cakes; cinnamon and peppermint oils to flavor homemade hard candies; and the rarest of all, a hard, brown, hairy coconut with its monkey face for the holiest of holies to grace a Shenandoah Valley Christmas table — a fresh coconut layer cake.

In a time when funds for gifts were limited, rural Shenandoah Valley families emphasized having an abundance of food on hand for the Christmas season. The bigger the family, the more cakes, cookies, pies, and candies were needed. Extra bags of flour, made from local wheat ground at Bear or Frank's Mill in Augusta County; Kline's Mill or Springdale Flour Mill in Frederick County; central Shenandoah County's Lantz Mill and Edinburg Mill; the Verbena or Willow Grove Mill in Page County; or perhaps Rockingham County's Arbogast, Stuckell's, or Silver Lake mills, were brought home for the marathon of baking that lay ahead. Greater amounts of the farm's eggs, butter, and cream — already dropping in quantity as winter approached — were set aside, reserved for the family's favorite recipes.

In Shenandoah Valley kitchens, housewives and their daughters raced to bake enough cookies between the usual cooking, cleaning, washing, ironing, and child care to fill at least one lard can before Christmas. Men and boys spent their evenings cracking black walnuts in the kitchen beside the woodstove, often eating as many of the nutmeats as they handed over for that week's baking. The baking progressed in a sequence — fruitcakes first, so they could be wrapped in cheese cloth to age and be splashed with bourbon; then the thin crisp sugar and ginger cookies cut in fancy shapes; followed by the softer lemon crackers, molasses cookies, and jumbles. The applesauce cakes and candies followed, with the pies and coconut cake made just before Christmas.

In the midst of the flurry of Christmas baking, children practiced their parts and pieces for the upcoming church pageant and, as the decades progressed, songs and recitations for the annual school Christmas program were added to these rehearsals. Elementary school activities during these years might include making red and green paper chains and Christmas cards or possibly even a small gift for parents; listening to teachers read selections from *Christmas in Legend and Story: A Book for Boys and Girls* (1915); and writing letters to Santa Claus to practice penmanship.

Christmas shopping, as we know it, was not a common practice, but children spent hours poring over the toy section in the Sears and Roebuck and Montgomery Ward mail order catalogs for hours, letting their imaginations run wild.

Like the school Christmas program, a Valley church Christmas pageant – always held the Sunday before Christmas – was a mixture of deepest solemnity and high festivity. A few days earlier, members of the church brought armloads of pine, running cedar, mountain laurel, and other greens to the church, built a fire in the great woodstoves, and set about decorating it for Christmas. Windowsills were filled with branches of pine and hemlock, stems of spiceberries, and streamers of running cedar artfully arranged around a wax candle carefully centered in each frosty window. In the front of the church, the altar or choir area was banked with great pine branches, while twigs of pine, cedar, and perhaps boxwood were snipped and tied together to fashion wreaths, garlands, and swags to decorate walls, ceiling, doors, and pews.

The pageant itself included the usual mixture of the

Julie Gochenour's childhood home

Christmas story from the Bible, children in fanciful and not-so-fanciful costumes acting out the familiar verses, and perhaps a dozen Christmas carols most members of the congregation could sing by heart. Church that morning or evening might then conclude with a Sunday School party complete with a Christmas tree. Some years in the Shenandoah Valley, lucky children received a tiny bag of hard candies or striped candy cane, but even in lean times there were always popcorn balls, plates of big fat cookies studded with raisins or walnuts, and at least a piece or two of homemade taffy or molasses candy to enjoy.

After the church Christmas pageant, Valley families finalized their own Christmas preparations. The first order of business was to find a Christmas tree. The task usually took at least half a day, with all but the smallest members of the family tramping across several fields before finding what seemed to be the perfect tree. There were, of course, no bought Christmas trees in those days. Instead, farm families found and cut their own while those who lived in town headed out to farms and fields owned by friends or family to do the same. Most families in the Shenandoah Valley chose the common, rather prickly but nicely shaped and readily available cedar trees. Other households, however, held out for a softer white pine, sometimes cutting the top out of larger trees to meet their needs.

Both pine and cedar trees were fragrant, but because cedars tended to dry out quickly, they were often not brought inside and put up and decorated until Christmas Eve. Decorations typically consisted of a few precious, fragile, thin, colored glass ornaments; tinsel or thin strips of silver-colored lead icicles; and some found treasures such as a bird's nest or clusters of scarlet rose hips. Other families wrapped poplar balls or walnut shells in gold or silver foil

Julie and her sister, Paula, with grandparents Dan and Martha Burner

salvaged from the inside of cigarette packages and pouches of chewing tobacco, or fashioned stars and diamonds from the same. The dried, prickly cedar tree with these decorations could be thrown out a few days later without a second thought.

Some families opened gifts on Christmas Eve, others on Christmas day, and a few even waited until Christmas night. As the legend of Santa Claus became widespread, Valley children began hanging stockings on Christmas Eve, but these were their own socks, and Santa usually filled them with such modest treats as an orange (or, later, a tangerine), a few mixed nuts in their exotic shells, and perhaps a candy cane. Many farm families made a point of putting down fresh bedding for the livestock and doing as much of the next day's work as possible on Christmas Eve. But while Christmas morning might come just once a year cows, pigs, and chickens still had to be fed, and many children on the Valley's family farms were forced to wait until the usual chores were finished before they could see the Christmas tree and receive their gifts.

But it was the Christmas dinner, not the Christmas tree, which was most often the center of a Shenandoah Valley farm family's attention. Families who could afford to do so saved back a country ham, butchered the previous winter, for their Christmas dinner while others had roast chicken or perhaps a turkey that had been killed, cleaned, and plucked a day or two earlier. These were often served with the rare treat of oysters that came to local grocers and merchants on trains from eastern Virginia. Oysters were a great luxury and Shenandoah Valley housewives typically shucked and stewed or fried these. Then they placed the oysters on the Christmas table at the very last possible moment, alongside the ham, poultry and a raft of homegrown vegetables such mashed potatoes, green beans, corn, sauerkraut, stewed tomatoes and homemade breads, biscuits, jams, jellies, apple butter, and pickles.

The days immediately after this Christmas were spent visiting family and friends, exchanging gifts of candies and cookies, and possibly entertaining "Belnicklers." These anonymous masked men were usually neighbors who disguised themselves and went from house to house seeking the hospitality that Christmastime promised all strangers and the bounty that continues to characterize a Shenandoah Valley Christmas to this day.

WILLIAM M. E. RACHAL

Christmas Dinner for Lee's Army

HUNGER WAS A CONSTANT COMPANION of General Robert E. Lee's soldiers in 1864. During the summer it was kept at arm's length, but when winter winds blew through tattered uniforms, a pint of corn meal and an ounce or two of bacon were not enough to ward off its pangs.

No one died of starvation, but the vitality of the Army of Northern Virginia was sapped. The lean Confederates were further annoyed by accounts of the Thanksgiving dinner enjoyed by the Federal soldiers who besieged Richmond and Petersburg that fall and early winter.

As Christmas approached, rumors of the feast in preparation for the Northerners made the prospect seem doubly barren for the Johnny Reb. There was little chance that the empty larder of the Confederate Commissary Department would provide a bountiful Christmas dinner.

Aroused by the privations of its valiant defenders, Richmonders determined to give Lee's veterans a feast at Christmas. The germ of the idea actually seems to have come from North Carolina, where plans were made to send the ingredients for Christmas dinner to the Tar Heel soldiers in the Army of Northern Virginia. However, once the citizens of Richmond adopted the idea, their enterprise transcended all others.

The original plan was to provide Christmas dinner for the Virginia troops defending Richmond, but the emphasis on state organizations was soon forgotten. The plan was expanded quickly to include all men in Lee's army. Indeed, it would have shown a want of gratitude to exclude any defender of Richmond from the feast. Later General Wade Hampton's cavalry, although they seemed constantly moving, were added to the dinner list.

A week before Christmas, Captain Richard F. Walker, manager of the Richmond Examiner, volunteered to receive contributions for the dinner. Others quickly joined the undertaking, and by December 21 about $50,000 had been raised, but four times that amount was sought. Members of the Virginia General Assembly and the Confederate Congress each contributed one day's pay, while George Trenholm, Confederate Secretary of the Treasury, subscribed $2,000. Later, an anonymous donor gave $5,000 to top Trenholm's handsome gift.

Four days before Christmas the need for an organization to carry the project to a successful conclusion was evident. Contractor John Enders and lawyers J. L. Apperson and Andrew Johnston were appointed at a meeting of Richmond citizens on December 21 to solicit subscriptions with the aid of subcommittees.

Apperson pointed out that there was not time enough remaining to prepare a Christmas dinner for so many and suggested that the feast be postponed until New Year's Day. As that holiday fell on Sunday, the dinner was eventually set for Monday, January 2, 1865.

The appeal for contributions for money and food was expanded, and John J. Wilson was designated to receive all gifts and, with others, to purchase provisions. The Southern Express Company offered to carry, free of charge, all presents to Lee's army for the Christmas dinner, and other Virginia railroads soon made similar offers.

Soon, Virginia women offered the treasures of their pantries. Hams, chickens, and turkeys came out of hiding. War had ravaged the state, but devotion supplied the ingredients for a feast. Nothing was too good or too scarce to be given to Lee's valiant veterans.

Money continued to come from various sources. Collections from houses along Main Street one day resulted in $5,290 collected in just two hours. A benefit theatrical production in Richmond on December 28 brought in more funds, while a student production in Petersburg was held on December 29 and other activities in that adjacent city accounted for $35,000 more for the dinner.

The task of cooking the enormous dinner got under way on December 27. Thomas Tyler left his duties in the Confederate States transportation office to superintend the preparation of the poultry and meats. A caterer with wide experience in the management of hotels, he was at home in the Ballard House hotel kitchen.

For some time those kitchens at Franklin and 14th streets had been unoccupied, but now, on the invitation of the proprietor, John P. Ballard, they became a hive of activity day and night. In the basement, hotel employees tended the boilers that supplied the kitchen's hot water, while others presided over the mammoth brick oven in the depths of which 300 fowls or pieces of meat could be baked every four hours.

On the hotel's second floor the kitchen range, formerly used to bake bread, glowed ruddily as it roasted turkeys. Nearby in kettles supplied with water from the basement, hams spent an hour boiling briskly.

Richmond's Ballard House Hotel

The Ballard House's veteran housekeeper presided over the arrangements. Under her direction, a retinue of servants dressed fowls, basted meats, and otherwise helped to prepare the feast. Nothing was wasted. Barrel after barrel was filled with grease from the cooked meats. Later, on behalf of the committee, Thompson Tyler sold about half a ton of this valuable byproduct to the Virginia Central Railroad for about $7,000, or $7 per pound.

When finally cooked, the meats were borne into the hotel's large barroom, where boiled hams and roasted pigs were piled high. Ducks, chickens, and turkeys were pyramided in small mountains, awaiting the carving knife. Over this treasury of tempting meats a guard of gentlemen kept watch night and day lest some visitor, overcome by his admiration of a turkey, should rob a soldier of a drumstick.

Although the meats on hand were judged to be sufficient to feed 30,000 or 40,000 men, Wilson continued to gather provisions up to the very last day.

Sixty barrels of flour were purchased and turned into 36,000 loaves of bread at the bakery of Pleasants and Frayser. Vegetables, which were collected in enormous quantities, were sent to the front uncooked, along with dried fruit, butter, and some of almost everything else which would enter into the composition of a good Christmas dinner.

On Sunday January 1, 1865, the meats were packed into

boxes and barrels for distribution the next day. Into each went an assortment embracing beef, ham, mutton, venison, shoat, fowl, and sausage, so that all companies would enjoy a variety. A special barrel was directed to "General R. E. Lee and Staff" near Petersburg.

Lee's staff opened the barrel when the general was away. The dozen or so turkeys it contained were arranged on a board placed on the snow. A large bird was flanked on each side by progressively smaller birds. Answering a staff summons, Lee rode up, dismounted, and joined his officers, who indicated that the big turkey belonged to him.

For a moment Lee stood, looking down at the tempting fowl, his unslung sword in his hand. Touching the big turkey with the scabbard, he said. "This, then, is my turkey? I don't know, gentlemen, what you are going to do with your turkeys, but I wish mine sent to the hospital in Petersburg so that some of the convalescents may have a good Christmas dinner."

Lee then mounted and rode away.

Without a word, his officers put the turkeys back into the barrel and sent it to the hospital.

The ambulance committee of Richmond was in charge of the distribution of the soldiers' dinner. Its job, however, was too great to be accomplished in a single day, so only part of the 30-mile-long Confederate line of the Army of Northern Virginia feasted on Monday. Other segments celebrated Tuesday.

Some parts of the army got plenty of food, while others got very little. But, for what they got the soldiers were truly thankful and blessed the good people of Richmond.

A veteran private wrote, "No better evidence of our thankfulness could be seen than to have witnessed our sturdy old veterans as they seated themselves at the banquet to gnaw upon the large, fat and juicy turkey legs; their sparkling eyes and deep-heaving breasts speaking louder than words."

The Angel of Marye's Heights

DURING THE CHRISTMAS SEASON, our thoughts turn toward angels and miracles as told in many of our favorite songs and stories, perhaps most importantly, the story of the original Christmas in Bethlehem.

Another story of the Christmas season, handed down from generation to generation, is one from December of 1862 as Union and Confederate troops battled in Fredericksburg during the Civil War.

That story focuses on Richard Rowland Kirkland, at the time of the Battle of Fredericksburg a young Confederate sergeant with Company G, 2nd Regiment, South Carolina Volunteer Infantry serving under Gen. Joseph B. Kershaw.

But years later, Kirkland became known as the "Angel of Marye's Heights," referring to the section of Fredericksburg where our story of the Christmas season takes place. And to many, Kirkland remains that angel.

In 1880, Kershaw wrote to the editor of the *News and Courier* newspaper in Charleston, S.C. about something that happened in December of 1862.

Let's look at that letter from 1880, attributed to Kershaw

but told in the third person, to learn the story. During the battle, the ground between the Union and Confederate lines was littered with the wounded, the dead and the dying. Their groans and cries filled the air, many of them calling for water.

Gen. Kershaw was upstairs in a home that bordered the area surveying the fighting. Kirkland came to the general with "an expression of indignant remonstrance."

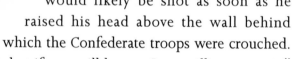

"General, I can't stand this," Kirkland said.

When Kershaw asked the young sergeant what was wrong, Kirkland replied, "All night and all day I have heard these poor people crying for water, and I can stand it no longer. I come to ask permission to go and give them water."

Kershaw warned Kirkland that he would likely be shot as soon as he raised his head above the wall behind which the Confederate troops were crouched.

Sgt. Richard Kirkland

"I know that; but if you will let me, I am willing to try it," the letter continues. "Kirkland, I ought not to allow you to run a risk, but the sentiment which actuates you is so noble that I will not refuse your request, trusting that God may protect you. You may go."

The sergeant asked permission to show a white handkerchief, but Kershaw denied that request. The young sergeant was determined to go ahead with his mission.

The letter continues:

"With profound anxiety he was watched as he stepped over the wall on his errand of mercy — Christ-like mercy. Unharmed, he reached the nearest sufferer. He knelt beside

him, tenderly raised the drooping head, rested it gently upon his own noble breast, and poured the precious life-giving fluid down the fever-scorched throat.

This done, he laid him tenderly down, placed his knapsack under his head, straightened out his broken limb, spread his overcoat over him, replaced his empty canteen with a full one, and turned to another sufferer.

By this time his purpose was well understood on both sides, and all danger was over. From all parts of the field arose fresh cries of "Water, water; for God's sake, water!" More piteous still the mute appeal of some who could only feebly lift a hand to say, here, too, is life and suffering.

For an hour and a half did this ministering angel pursue his labor of mercy, nor ceased to go and return until he relieved all the wounded on that part of the field. He returned to his post wholly unhurt. Who shall say how sweet his rest that winter's night beneath the cold stars!"

Young Kirkland didn't survive the war but did endure two major battles following Fredericksburg. With his regiment, under Kershaw's Brigade, he participated in battles at Chancellorsville in May and at Gettysburg, July 1–3, 1863. During Gettysburg as his outfit participated in the clash in the Peach Orchard and adjacent Wheatfield, Kirkland distinguished himself again through his ability and personal acts of courage. Those efforts led to his promotion to lieutenant.

As part of Lieutenant General James Longstreet's Corps, Kershaw's Brigade and thus Kirkland were transferred from the Army of Northern Virginia to the Army of Tennessee in the late summer of 1863. He ultimately died on September 30, 1863 after leading a charge in the battle's waning hours. Realizing that he had advanced too far ahead of the rest of the troops, he and his men tried to return to their own company. He was shot,

Kirkland Monument on Fredericksburg Battlefield

along with several others; his last words reportedly were: "I am done for, save yourselves …and please tell my pa I died right."

Kershaw noted the young soldier's death in his letter, but he concluded with this:

> "He was but a youth when called away, and had never formed those ties from which might have resulted in a posterity to enjoy his fame and bless his country; but he has bequeathed to the American youth — yea, to the world — an example which dignifies our common humanity."

Kershaw's 1880 letter to a newspaper — almost two decades after the Battle of Fredericksburg — is the basis for this angel "legend."

The story has led to a major sculpted statue erected in the location which is part of the Fredericksburg and Spotsylvania National Military Park. The sculptor is Felix de Weldon, the same artist who created the statue for the Iwo Jima Memorial. The sculpture shows one man leaning over another, offering him a drink from his canteen.

There have been countless words written about the story; there was even a half-hour dramatic documentary in 2010 telling the story.

Some people support the story as an accurate portrayal of events. While there have not appeared any officers' reports or other writings from the Battle of Fredericksburg citing Kirkland's extraordinary exhibition of courage and compassion, there have been stories from other battles where soldiers from one side showed their humanity by tending to the wounded from the opposition.

Others simply discount this tale as fiction. They point to those battle reports and argue that something that stopped the intense fighting for 90 minutes would certainly have been included.

For people who look through the eyes of historians, perhaps there needs to be definitive documentation one way or another.

But for many, and this may be especially true in the season of Christmas, does it really matter?

Maybe we all would like to think we have a little of Richard Kirkland inside us, hoping that if the situation arose we could be brave enough, and humane enough, to care for our fellow human being at such a critical time of need.

Isn't that what the holiday spirit is all about?

Christmas on the Eastern Shore

VIRGINIANS WHO GREW UP in cities probably have fond memories of venerable department stores such as Thalhimer's and Miller and Rhoads, where Christmas became a magical time for children. But on Virginia's Eastern Shore, memories are more likely wrapped up in the senses rather than material things, and they are likely to be associated with the land, and certainly with the bays, creeks, and marshes that surround us.

On the Eastern Shore the only "real" Christmas tree is the eastern red cedar, a native that grows wild and is especially fond of swampy places where the upland and the salt marsh meet. We would pick one out long before Christmas, probably as we were trudging through the woods with the bird dog during hunting season. We would cut it with a hand saw, pressing into the fragrant base of the tree, feeling the little pricks of cedar spurs, having them fall under the jacket collar and down the neck. We would drag it out of the woods and drive it home in the back of the truck, and then put it up in the living room, where it would lend its cedar scent to the entire house, mixing now and then with the aroma of country ham, sweet potato biscuits, and

71

salted fish slow-cooking in a cast-iron skillet. Some years the tree would have a cocoon hidden within the branches, and after a few days of warmth, we'd find our gift of miniature praying mantises among the presents beneath the tree.

The tree was like a member of the family for a fortnight or so, until the sweetness of Christmas played out and we returned to schools and jobs and the Christmas toys went into the box in the closet with last year's toys. And then the lights and decorations would be gathered and stored and the old tree, dry and crisp, would be dragged across the room, leaving a trail of cedar spurs, and it would go out into the yard and under the bird feeder. There it would stay until the grass needed mowing in late March or early April, and all this time it would support a family of white-throated sparrows that would forage spilled sunflower seeds and sing their plaintive song.

I mentioned salted fish. When Virginia was a colony, the combination of salt and fish kept the early settlers alive. The fish provided protein and the salt would preserve the fish for months. So the sea trout and bluefish caught during the fall could, possibly, prevent starvation and disease during the cold winter months when fresh fish were not available. My grandparents had a refrigerator, but still they salted fish. So did my parents. Me too.

Salting fish, once a matter of survival, is now a part of the Christmas ritual. Christmas breakfast consists of scrambled eggs, bacon, biscuits with fig preserves, and a fillet of fish, slowly boiled in water, topped with a medallion of butter.

I suppose I enjoy the tradition of salting fish as much as I enjoy eating them. It's a process that links the generations, one that is unchanged since the time of the colonists. Our old stone crock has been used for so many years for salting fish that the salt has leached through the glazing and into the clay. No matter how many times you wash it, a white filigree of salt will decorate the dark inner walls of the container as soon as it dries.

We go out in late October, while the bays and creeks still have a few spot, croakers, and trout. I prepare the fish by scaling and filleting them, then rinsing them in fresh water to remove blood, which causes the fish to spoil. Then I pack them in a crock of salt. A layer of salt, a layer of fish. And so on until I run out of fillets. I cover the crock with a tea towel, place a dinner plate on top to hold it, and let the fish and the salt begin their chemical reaction, a marriage of earth and sea, holding in suspension the last of the summer as we await a new spring.

In a few weeks the fish and the salt will make a brine, and the fish will become firmer and the meat will be opaque. If we anticipate a Sunday breakfast of fish, we'll take a few fillets out on Saturday, let them soak in fresh water overnight, and boil them in water in the iron skillet in the morning. A little butter and black pepper are the only seasonings necessary.

❄   ❄   ❄

The Christmas Brant

THE RELATIONSHIP of Christmas to the land and sea around us is vividly expressed in a story by Alexander Hunter, published in his book *The Huntsman in the South* (Neale, 1908). Hunter spent the Christmas of 1905 on Hog Island, a barrier island along the Virginia coast that at the time had a village of about 200 people. Hunter went to Hog Island to go waterfowl hunting and was the guest of Charles Sterling, the keeper of the lighthouse.

A few days before Christmas, Hunter was sleeping soundly in the lighthouse keeper's cottage. Around midnight, someone began pounding on the door. It was Charles Sterling, and he wanted Hunter to come at once to the nearby lighthouse. An incredible event was taking place.

A gale had been brewing all day, so Hunter put on his oilskins and left the cottage with Sterling, both men leaning hard into the wind and sleet. They climbed the circular stairway to the keeper's room just beneath the light, and then went out onto a narrow iron balcony, icy with rain and sleet. Thousands of brant, buffeted by the storm, had been attracted to the light. Many crashed into the glass, stunned, some falling lifeless to the ground below. "The brant, the shyest, wildest, most timid of waterfowl, were within five feet of us, but, evidently blinded by the light, they could see nothing," Hunter wrote. "Some would circle around the tower, others dart by; and wonderful to relate, some would remain stationary in the air, their wings moving so rapidly that they were blurred like a wheel in rapid motion. The lamp in the tower revolved every forty-five seconds, and for a short time every bird was in the vivid glare, which displayed every graceful curve of neck and head, and the set and balance of the body, and enabled one to look into their brilliant eyes."

Soon, many of the people who lived on the island had heard of the event, and they gathered with their dogs in the lighthouse compound, collecting dead brant and dispatching the wounded. Some men wanted access to the lighthouse balcony so they could shoot the brant, but Sterling refused. Sterling himself picked up 28 brant, Hunter wrote, the villagers many times that number.

Hunter's account of the incident in *The Huntsman in the South* illustrates the gulf that had developed between people whose ancestors viewed wildlife as a means of subsistence and those who view it as sport. To Hunter the event was tragic, and the villagers' actions were savage. But to the villagers it was serendipitous. The winter weather had been harsh, the fishing season was over, and times were hard for everyone. But Christmas was coming, and because of the event that night, tragic though it was, there would be a Christmas feast for all.

TRADITIONS

A Colonial Christmas

Christmas is come, hang on the pot,
Let spits turn 'round, and ovens be hot;
Beef, pork and poultry, now provide
To feast thy neighbors at this tide;
Then wash all down with good wine and beer,
And so with mirth conclude the Year.
                    – *Virginia Almanack, 1765*

VIRGINIA, OF ALL THE COLONIES in early America, kept closer ties to the Mother Country – in laws, social life and holiday customs.

Whether it be sleigh bells ringing, children singing, Yule logs aglow, toy-filled stockings hanging by the hearth, holly wreaths on the front door, mistletoe in the hallway or carol singers going door to door, there is an English Christmas feeling in many of the homes today in Virginia, just as there was in the colonial era with those traditions carried down through the years.

During the interregnum of Protector Oliver Cromwell (1648–1660) when the monarchy was terminated, England was forced to abandon Christmas and one could get into deep trouble for attending a Christmas service, as did diarist John Evelyn. On Christmas Day 1657, in London, he and his wife were arrested while receiving the sacrament, musket-pointing Puritan soldiers threatening them "as if they would have shot us at the altar."

It was seen that way in Puritan Massachusetts. A law enacted in 1659 read: "Whosoever shall be found observing any such day as Christmas, or the like, either by forbearing of labor, or feasting in any other way, shall be fined 5 shillings, and forbade the Festival of Christmas and kindred ones, superstitiously kept." The law was only in effect for 22 years, but Christmas was not made a legal holiday in Massachusetts until the mid-19th century.

The Puritan order of Cromwell's England was minimized in Virginia, but those traditions lost for a few years were rekindled when the monarchy returned. In 1680 a French guest attending the home of Colonel William Fitzhugh in Fredericksburg during the Christmas season wrote, "There was good wine and all kinds of beverages, so there was a great deal of carousing," and the colonel hired "three fiddlers, a jester, a tight-rope walker, and an acrobat who tumbled around" for entertainment.

Was Fitzhugh the Christmas exception or the rule? We do not know, because there are few existing holiday accounts of colonial Virginia Christmas celebrations. In fact, 100 years later diarist John Harrower, wrote from Belvedere Plantation, also near Fredericksburg, on Christmas Day 1774 that he had "no saddle on which to ride to church" for Sunday services.

Another diarist, Philip Vickers Fithian, said "Guns fired all around the House" awakened him on Christmas morn 1773 at Nomini Hall in Westmoreland County where he resided in the home of Robert Carter, the scion of one of Virginia's wealthiest and most influential families. Later in the day, Fithian handed out sixpences to the servants that cost him three shillings and a ha'penny, modest largesse then described as a Christmas box. But that was about the extent of Fithian's giving or receiving. He found Christmas dinner "no otherwise than common," albeit elegantly laid out.

The Christmas Day entry of a much earlier diarist, William Byrd of Westover in Charles City County, recalled that in 1740 it was too cold for him to go to church, though he did have roast turkey on the table.

Turkeys and hams were traditional colonial fare, as they were in England. Even in the midst of a hot and sickly summer, a Yorktown resident thought to ship two "Christmas turkeys" to London, saying, "Mrs. Mary Ambler will send hams to eat with them." But that was about as Christmassy as colonial Virginians became.

In short, an 18th-century Christmas, be it in Virginia, or in the Royal Court in London, was primarily a religious festival – as it was meant to be. Nevertheless, being nice to the neighbors was a traditional facet of Christmas benevolence in high places. In 1772 the *Virginia Gazette* reported that at Windsor Lodge, the Duke of Cumberland kept "open table for the Country People, for three Days, covered with Surloins of roast Beef, Plum Puddings, and minced Pies, the rich and ancient Food of Englishmen." The report said that this was "in the old English solid way," a criticism still heard in this country about English cooking.

In 1774 Christmas fell conveniently on a Sunday, and amid

much regal pomp George III and Queen Charlotte received the sacrament in the Chapel-Royal from the hands of the Lord Bishop of London, assisted by the Lord Bishop of Chichester and the Clerk of the King's Closet. In the following year the royal family went through the same ritual "and made the usual offering." The reporting newspaper noted, however, "the day has been kept with more strictness, by all ranks of people in this metropolis, than for some years past."

One immediately wonders what level of laxity had been perceived in previous years. It was, however, far more likely that antisocial behavior blossomed in the day *after* Christmas, that being the occasion for masters to reward servants and apprentices with ceramic money boxes containing their annual bonuses, which quickly went down their throats in the nearest taverns.

As early as 1387 Geoffrey Chaucer wrote about the apprentice, his box, and his reputation for wild and riotous behavior. Although it is doubtful that any happy apprentice gave a thought to the origins of Boxing Day, the church was all too aware that the day of giving and receiving gifts could be traced to the pagan Roman Saturnalia, an event unfit for pious eyes or ears.

Although there is evidence that the stroke of a Puritanical pen outlawed many an old English custom thought to have had pagan origins, in the tradition-shrouded recesses of the countryside such edicts were contemptuously ignored. Albeit in distorted forms, therefore, some traditions survived to be absorbed into the Christmas we still enjoy. Take, for example, the Yule log. In the medieval centuries, when candles were expensive and hearths wide, the notion that the birth of the Christ child became the light of the world was reflected in the Christmas Eve burning of a large, knotted, and slow-burning log or wooden block.

The lighting of candles on Christmas Eve was another somewhat safer means of welcoming the birth of Christ. In the sixteenth century, and probably earlier, single, very large candles called specifically "Christmas candles" were burned in churches and in homes, and it is this tradition of welcoming the infant Jesus with candles that has continued in many churches today as prelude to the sacred day.

Decorating one's home with ivy and other greenery was another tradition whose roots were dug deep in pagan Europe and were yet another feature of the Roman Saturnalia that stretched from December 17 to 24. Created as a celebration for Saturnus, the god of agriculture, it evolved into an all-you-can-think-of festival of unbridled joy, with the warding off of evil spirits and the celebrating of new growth. Later Christian representations were given to them: The holly represented Christ's crown of thorns he wore at his crucifixion, and the berries represented his drops of blood shed for all. The ivy must cling to something to support its growth, reminding all of the need to cling to God for daily support.

The fir we cut to stand in the living-room corner may stem from the same classical sources, though most of the myths surrounding it are Germanic — as College of William and Mary professor Charles Frederick Ernest Minnigerode well knew. He joined the faculty in 1842 to teach Latin and Greek and brought his native *weihnachtsbaum* (Christmas tree) tradition with him. He set it up in the Courthouse Green home of his lawyer friend Beverley Tucker. It was not until Christmas Eve 1915, however, that the City of Williamsburg chose Palace Green to erect its first public illuminated tree. The tradition continues, though it has shifted to Market Square Green (old Courthouse Green).

It is not known if the Minnigerode tree had lighted candles on its branches, but within a few years the flickering candlelight bedecked many a Christmas tree. Today, of course, few of us risk using anything but electric candles, and the traditional white lights have now gone multi-colored and flicker alternating colors and even to the beat of various holiday tunes.

Like candles, fire has always been at the heart of Christmas. In pre-Christian Germany, in houses where smoke escaped through a hole in the roof rather than up a chimney, the winter solstice was dedicated to Hertha, the goddess of domesticity. The room was decked with evergreens and a great fire was laid on a large, flat altar stone set in the center. In the midst of feasting, the goddess would descend through the smoke to bestow good luck on the host and his guests. Thus, according to some mythologists, the Hertha stone became our hearthstones, and the legend explains why, rather than entering in a reasonable and civilized way, Santa Claus comes down the chimney.

And what about carols? Christmas without carolers would be like – well, like holly without ivy. The word is said to derive from the Latin *cantare*, to sing, and *rola*, an expression of joy, and its earliest surviving text dates from the 13th century. But caroling being a monastic activity, it fell into disfavor in the reign of Henry VIII, later to be revived in more secular forms only to be condemned by the Puritans.

By the time the British got over that hurdle, old-style carols were considered antiquated. Consequently, it was not until the 19th century that most of the carols we now sing were written. "Silent Night" was first published in 1840, "Hark the Herald Angels Sing" in 1856, "O Come, All Ye Faithful" was not translated into English until 1841, and "O Little Town of Bethlehem" was written for a Philadelphia Sunday School in 1868.

But remarkably, one American tradition — Santa Claus — has found its way to England. Until the mid-1950s the deliverer of children's Christmas gifts in Britain was known as Father Christmas. Originally developing from St. Nicholas, he moved through parishes with a bit of a religious tone — a kind of medieval social worker. Later, all the saintly and religious elements were lost, but the figure remained as a "benevolent, jovial character, synonymous with the Goodwill of Christmas" and kept people happy at a dismal, dark wintry time of year.

But by the late nineteenth century, he became a fat, jolly character who filled children's stockings in the early hours of Christmas Day. His old robe with his head bedecked in a holly wreath gave way to a figure with a white beard, red coat and pants, and a great fur-trimmed hat. The American Santa had arrived.

At Christmas play and make good cheer,
For Christmas comes but once a year.

Good bread and good drink, a good fire in the hall,
Brawn, pudding and souse, and good mustard withall:
Beef, mutton and pork, shred pies of the best:
Pig, veal, goose and capon and turkey well drest:
Cheese, apples and nuts, jolly carols to hear,
As then in the country is counted good cheer.

— Thomas Tusser, 1573

E80365 1975

Miller & Rhoads
RICHMOND, VA.

Miller & Rhoads's Legendary Santa

I BELIEVED IN SANTA CLAUS for a long time. A *very* long time. Far longer than most kids.

Why? Because each year at Christmastime, I saw the "real" Santa. And the real Santa was not your average mall Santa. The real Santa knew my name.

Well-known to native Richmonders like myself, Legendary Santa was a staple at the former Miller & Rhoads department store in the heart of the city's downtown district from my mother's post-WWII childhood right through my own youth. And for decades, children traveled far and wide, from Virginia and beyond, to see him.

Upon Santa's arrival, the entire city was resplendent in Christmas decor. Extravagant holiday window displays adorned storefronts lining the streets of downtown. Bruce the Spruce, a cheeky talking Christmas tree, never ceased to fascinate me. And the entire seventh floor of Miller & Rhoads – normally vacant storage space – was transformed into a magical wonderland. *Santa Land.*

This was downtown Richmond in its prime. And every year my family was there to experience it.

Since lines for Legendary Santa were infamously long on the weekends, my parents took my little brother and me out of school each year to see him. This was a special treat.

Dressed in our Sunday best, we'd head downtown on a December afternoon and watch in awe as Santa came down the chimney to take his place on his gilded chair. Then we would wait not-so-patiently in line for our turn to sit on his lap, requiring my poor, beleaguered mother to intermittently smooth our rumpled clothing, lest we look like a pair of bedraggled street urchins by the time we greeted Santa.

But first came a chat with his Snow Queen – an ethereal young woman who always struck me as incredibly sophisticated even though, in hindsight, she couldn't have been more than 20.

Next, we would have our picture taken with Santa himself. By an elf. Despite the absurdity of this, my mom still has every picture we ever took with Santa Claus.

Afterward, we would dine with Santa and his entourage in the renowned Miller & Rhoads Tea Room while watching famed Richmond performer Eddie Weaver play Christmas tunes on the organ, piano, or quite often, both at the same time.

But the highlight of these annual excursions downtown was our visit with Santa himself. Because the true magic of Legendary Santa – the thing that made him so *real* – lay in the fact that he somehow knew every child's name.

As we waited our turn with the Snow Queen, my brother and I would watch with anticipation as Santa waved goodbye to his previous charges and turned his attention toward us. "*Kristin and Justin!*" he would bellow. "*Come on over here and see 'ol Santa!*"

To a child, that moment defined the magic of Christmas. *Santa knew my name.*

Miller & Rhoads is gone now. It went out of business in

1990, along with its neighbor and friendly rival, Thalhimer's.

The closing of both stores dealt a blow to downtown's consumer center, which, despite several revitalization attempts, never quite recovered. The area fell into disrepair and Christmastime in downtown Richmond was no longer a resplendent affair. Where holiday window displays once delighted city-goers, now there are mostly boarded-up storefronts – a sad reminder of what used to be.

And at some point, I stopped believing in Santa Claus.

I'm not quite sure when it happened; I think it was a gradual process. During one particular lunch in the Tea Room, for instance, I sat quietly, carefully studying the Santa dining in front of me, comparing him to the Santa on whose lap I had just sat.

"He has a different *nose,*" I announced, eyeing Imposter Santa suspiciously.

That was the end of lunch with Santa in the Tea Room. Yes, my parents went to great lengths to keep the magic alive.

Miller & Rhoads store decorated for Christmas

Then there was that fateful day in fifth grade when true skepticism took over. For after bragging that I'd be leaving school early that day to go see Santa Claus, a beady-eyed, freckle-faced kid named Owen said to me, "You know Santa's not *real*, right?"

And the seeds of doubt began to take root.

Thanks a lot, Owen.

By the time I turned 13, I was pretty sure a fat man in a red suit didn't break into our house in the middle of the night to bestow us with gifts; and I was fairly certain all the presents wrapped in Santa's "signature" gift wrap had actually come from my parents. Especially since the tags bore my mom's unmistakable immaculate handwriting.

And what of Santa Claus knowing my name? Sadly, I had begun to suspect he was wearing an earpiece connected to a hidden microphone worn by the Snow Queen. And while I'm neither confirming nor denying that this was the case, it would certainly explain why she was constantly repeating my name in an oddly emphasized fashion.

Logic applied to the fantastical quickly strips it of its magic; this was the first of several difficult truths I would learn as I transitioned from childhood to young adult. Nevertheless, I was a traditional child. And so at the age of 13, I again went to see Santa Claus, even though it felt silly at that point.

It would be my last visit with him.

For whatever reason, we didn't go the following year. And the year after that, Miller & Rhoads closed its doors for good. I grew up, moved away from Richmond, and got married. And as the years passed, caught up in holiday stress, I remembered less and less of why I once loved Christmas so much.

Legendary Santa, meanwhile, meandered aimlessly around Richmond in the years following Miller & Rhoads's closure. But these days, he has a new fitting home at the Children's

Museum of Richmond.

In 2010, my family and I spent Christmas in Richmond where I visited Legendary Santa for the first time since 1988 – this time with my year-old daughter. It marked the third generation of family excursions to see the "real" Santa Claus in downtown Richmond – in the 1950s, my Nana had taken my mother and aunt to visit him each year as well.

I was thrilled to be able to continue such a meaningful holiday tradition with my own daughter, and hope she'll grow to love it as much as I did.

Suddenly, I believe in Santa Claus again.

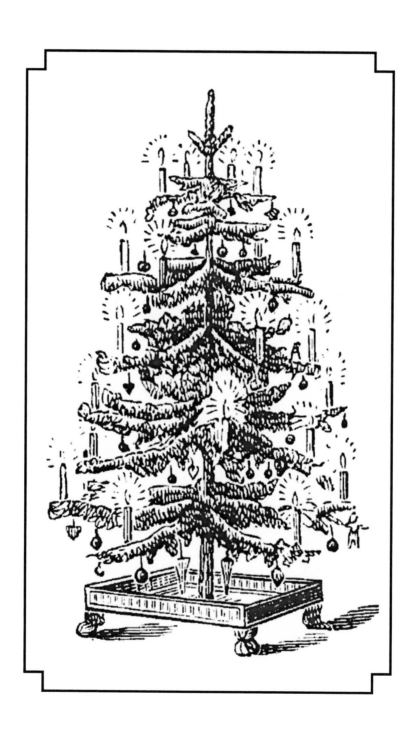

Virginia's First Christmas Tree

D R. JANET COLEMAN KIMBROUGH was a history buff who lived amid the past. She delighted in maintaining a longtime Virginia tradition in the St. George Tucker House in Williamsburg, the home of the Commonwealth's first Christmas tree. Every Christmas, for about half a century, Dr. Kimbrough lovingly had a cedar tree placed in the front hallway of that same 18th-century house to continue the custom begun there in 1842, when her grandmother, Cynthia Beverley Tucker, was a child. For it was at the Tucker House that the Williamsburg tree became legendary.

It was without a doubt the first Christmas tree in Williamsburg and the earliest known tree in Virginia – and quite possibly the first "family" tree in the country.

Until she died in 1992 at age 90, Dr. Kimbrough, a retired physician, enjoyed inviting her family, children of her family's friends, and other children from the community to a great party each Christmas holiday to see her tree and enjoy some of Williamsburg's holiday traditions.

My wife's family were longtime friends of the Tucker/ Coleman/Kimbrough clan, and when our daughter was born we began to be included in the holiday festivities at the Tucker House. I recall that children would enjoy playing around the Christmas tree with all sorts of old playthings, including wind-up tin toys 50 or more years old. They were the type of playthings that most of the children had never seen.

During one party Dr. Kimbrough joined the children at the tree. Sitting in a rocking chair, she told them the story she heard from her grandmother many years earlier of Virginia's first Christmas tree.

She was the great-granddaughter of Nathaniel Beverley Tucker, judge and law professor at the College of William and Mary, who in 1842 invited Charles Frederick Ernest Minnigerode to erect a German-style Christmas tree.

While living in Philadelphia, Minnigerode noticed an advertisement in a newspaper for a position to teach ancient languages at William and Mary.

He faced strong opposition from 30 other well-qualified applicants. Regarding his eventual appointment, a member of the college's board of visitors wrote:

> Testimonials of about thirty candidates were examined...

> The overwhelming certificates, letters of recommendation and evidences of qualification, of splendid attainments and other requisites for a professor, were so overpowering, that it left not a doubt or hesitancy in the minds of the visitors as to a choice, and on the first ballot Minnigerode was elected.

> He is one of the best educated men in this country, and Unsurpassed as a Classicist, writing Hebrew, Greek, & Latin with perfect ease & elegance.

Minnigerode became close friends with Judge Tucker, the law professor with whom he boarded.

"Minck," as he was nicknamed by the judge's children, was fond of his adopted Virginia home, but when the holiday season arrived, the German scholar longed for his homeland and its holiday customs and traditions.

Minck asked Tucker if he could give a party for the children – a German Christmas. The judge agreed, but little did he know that later he would be walking through the woods hunting for a tree to place in the parlor for his new German friend's Christmas party.

The two men went into the woods one afternoon to select a tree appropriate for the Tucker parlor and chose a small evergreen, cut it down, and brought it home.

The elaborate glass ornaments and tinseled globes of the German tree were not available in Virginia, so Minnigerode and the children fashioned ornaments from gilded nuts, strings of popcorn, and colored paper. Stubs of candles were wired to the tree branches, and tiny baskets of bonbons also were hung. A gilded crown was affixed to the top of the tree.

On Christmas Eve, in 1842, and every year afterward until the judge's death, a Christmas tree party was given for the children of friends and neighbors at the Tucker House on

The St. George Tucker House, where the first Virginia tree was decorated

courthouse green (now known as Market Square Green).

By 1843, the word of Minck's Christmas tree had spread through town, and indoor trees began to be lit by the Tucker neighbors and friends.

Even though the Kimbrough family no longer lives in the big house, a Christmas tree is annually put up in the Tucker House. Now owned by The Colonial Williamsburg Foundation, the home carefully maintains the rich tradition that encompasses at least 170 years.

Williamsburg has a hand in another Christmas tree tradition. It was the first city or town in Virginia and one of the early communities in the United States, probably one of the first 20 to 25, to begin a community tree lighting holiday tradition.

Two communities on opposite coasts of the United States – Perkasle, a small community in Bucks County, Pennsylvania, and Pasadena, California – apparently were the initial community

Williamsburg's Community Tree

tree celebrants as citizens gathered outdoors to revel in the festivities surrounding the grand lighting of the trees with incandescent bulbs.

Three years later, the community Christmas tree idea caught on in New York City, thanks to Emilie D. Lee Herreshoff, whose ancestors hailed from Bucks County. She took her idea to New York Mayor William J. Gaynor, who embraced the suggestion.

Ultimately, Madison Square Park was selected as the site, a 63-foot balsam fir was donated, and 1,200 incandescent lights were strung on it; it was called the "Tree of Light," according to the 1918 *New York Times*. A community tree also was lighted that year in Cleveland, Ohio.

The next year – 1913 – Philadelphia citizens erected their own community Christmas tree. *The Philadelphia Record* on December 25, 1913, reported the event held near Independence Hall.

On Christmas night 1915, Williamsburg residents gathered around a large evergreen on Palace Green to await the grand lighting. A newspaper reported:

> *When the bells begin to ring, all of Williamsburg will assemble on Palace Green to sing carols and hear the exercises that have been prepared for the community tree.*

The next year the Williamsburg event was moved to the west end of Duke of Gloucester Street to be near the college, the source of electrical power in the town at the time. But World War I caused the celebration to be suspended for a number of years until the custom was revived in 1933. This ceremony produced by the Williamsburg Civil League – a group of local religious and civic organizations – was held at a tree down a hillside from the old Capitol site and near the old debtor's prison.

In 1935, after the Colonial Williamsburg restoration had been formally in operation for about a year, the community Christmas tree celebration was held in conjunction with a variety of holiday activities in the city's newly proclaimed Historic Area.

Today, the community Christmas tree has spread to towns and cities across Virginia and the United States and has become a well-loved tradition encompassing a vast array of Yuletide themes and legends. In Williamsburg, hundreds of area citizens still gather on the edge of Market Square Green on Christmas Eve for the renewal of the city's tree lighting tradition.

Richmond's Nativity Pageant

OR MORE THAN 80 YEARS, wise men have brought
gold, frankincense, and myrrh – and a Christmas holiday
tradition – to Richmond, Virginia.

Since 1924, the age-old story of the birth of Jesus Christ
– The Nativity – has been re-created annually in a 30-minute
outdoor interdenominational drama, told by a narrator and choir.
It is produced on the steps of the Carillon in Byrd Park, with
a 50-member choir and a 250-member cast and crew on the
evening of December 23.

The Richmond Nativity Pageant, one of the city's oldest
holiday traditions, began on the steps of the State Capitol. Soon,
however, the crowds grew so large it was moved to the lawn of
the Capitol, and the stage was built over a fountain at the foot
of the hill. The sloping lawn became the hillside overlooking
Bethlehem. The pageant remained at the Capitol through 1942,
after which it was suspended from 1943–1945 because of
World War II.

After the war, the pageant moved to the Carillon, an
elaborate bell tower built as a memorial to those who died
in World War I. There are seven years when the pageant was

not held: the years during World War II and when storms forced cancellations.

In recent years, Larry Robinson, the carilloneur, plays traditional Christmas music on the Carillon bells for 30 minutes before the pageant. Everyone knows when he begins to play "Greensleeves," the program, in all its glory, is about to start.

Our family home is within a few blocks of the Carillon, and this story has become an important part of our lives. For my father, Bob Lovelace, Christmas was the most important time of the year and The Nativity Pageant was a great love of his. Every year he built a life-size nativity scene in our front yard. My grandfather started this tradition when my father was a young boy. On the night of the pageant, people would leave the program and stop by our house to see his display.

Four generations of my family have participated. My sister and brothers and I joined the cast around 1970 as People of Bethlehem. Throughout the years, I worked my way up to the coveted Angel loft. I portrayed Mary in 1982 and also became engaged to my husband that night. All three of our daughters have been Mary: Caitlyn in 2005, Victoria in 2008, and Anne Miflin in 2009. They now are back with the Angels on High.

Our participation is not unusual. Other families, like ours, have participated either as part of the cast or crew of the pageant for dozens of years, thus creating their own holiday traditions.

The Hudert family can proudly claim more than 30 members who have been part of the pageant, with the majority of them still very active. The Farley family of three brothers and three sisters and their children participate in the pageant. Three generations of the Martin family have been involved and brought other families to our program from the Ashland community. The Thiebaults drive to Richmond from Williams- burg to fulfill their family's tradition of being in the pageant.

Well-known historian and newspaper editor Douglas Southall Freeman wrote the original script and served as the first narrator until World War II. That script is still used today. Mr. Freeman stepped down from his role after the war, and his nephew G. Mallory Freeman took up the task and served until 1993. Then his son, Allen Freeman, became the narrator.

Mallory used to talk about his family holiday tradition of participating in the pageant, then going to a family holiday gathering afterward. All of his children and grandchildren grew up in The Nativity.

The year before Allen Freeman became narrator, he watched the performance and felt it was "very moving, very beautiful and very simple, with just words from the gospels and singing. It's not so grandiose as to be overwhelming in its pageantry, but it's large enough to inspire awe."

Like Allen, attendees are amazed by the reverence and serenity of the performance. The lights go up, the choir sings, and the People of Bethlehem begin their journey. You can hear a pin drop until the star in the East appears at the top of the Carillon tower as the pageant ends. As people leave, you can hear the comments about how moved they were, how glad that they came, how they would not miss this event ever again, and that it is now a part of their family tradition.

While some people stay in the same role for years, others grow up with the Nativity. They literally progress from the infant Jesus, to cherub, then on to a shepherd or a Roman soldier, and maybe even to one of the principal roles. The teenage girls in the pageant are always asking, "When can I be Mary?" As young ladies reach their late teens, we like to be able to have a father and daughter cast in the roles of Mary and Joseph. This means so much to the families.

For example, Adam Atwell was baby Jesus in 1991 and later was a member of the Bethlehem crowd, a shepherd, a Roman soldier and later Joseph. His mother Jennifer Holland was the baby Jesus in 1969 and now holds the coveted role as the lead shepherd angel.

Norbert Bliley, part of the Bliley Funeral Home family, portrayed a shepherd for nearly 30 years and has been pageant chairman for the last 11 years. His family, along with brother Nick Bliley and his family, have been huge supporters of the pageant for generations.

Carey Biley, son of Norbert, began his pageant career as a cherub and later became a shepherd. When he married his wife, Jenny, they became Mary and Joseph for a year, and their first son, Josh, was the baby Jesus several years ago.

Vicky Ellis Gates began participating in The Nativity with her mother, Terry Sprinkle, and father, Gary Ellis, about 38 years ago. She portrayed Mary in 1993 and, after she married, her new husband, Jay Gates, and his family joined the extended pageant family. One son, Brandt, was the baby Jesus in 2003, and he and her other son, Zane, now are two of the travelers.

I could go on and on with more family stories but you can tell how important this pageant has become to many individuals and families. We are a pageant family as well. The traditions instilled in each member are a part of who we are and what the pageant represents.

Often, people who have moved away come back either to see the production or to perform in another role. One couple, for a long time, drove down from Canada every other year – the production was that meaningful to them.

Dwayne Marsh, son of State Sen. Henry L. Marsh III and his wife, Diane, from Richmond, lived in California for many years and returned every Christmas to participate with us. His first performance was as a cherub in the early 1970s. His parents were former cast members.

Unfortunately, he has not been able to join us in recent years, but he laughingly told a reporter one time, "Assignments aren't just based on your tremendous acting ability. It may be what costume you fit into."

Jack Irwin was a cast member from 1946 until his retirement in 2010. He used to brag that he was the oldest cast member and "could remember way back when." I had known Jack since I was 10 years old and it was sad to lose our dear innkeeper. He did, however, return in 2011 to see the pageant and said he had never realized how beautiful the pageant really was.

From 1924 until 1985, the Richmond Department of Recreation and Parks sponsored The Nativity. However, in 1985 the legal question of separation of church and state arose within the country, and the community and the city department withdrew its support. Then Mayor Roy W. West and Councilwoman Geline B. Williams publicly expressed their disappointment that the sponsorship had to end.

The Richmond Jaycees became sponsors for one year in 1986. Subsequently, a foundation was created to raise an endowment to sponsor The Nativity annually. In 2002, the Christmas Eve performance was moved to December 23 because so many churches had Christmas Eve services and members of our choir and cast wanted to be at their home churches. As a result of changing the date, past participants returned to the pageant family, our audiences increased greatly, and new participants also have joined us.

A great deal of work goes into our pageant every year to bring the miracle of Christ's birth to the hearts and minds of our audiences. To hear from people that our pageant is "The true meaning of Christmas and the holiday season" makes all the effort worthwhile. I am so grateful to our Advisory Committee and all the supporting volunteers each year that make this production so tremendous. Once the pageant ends and costumes are being stowed for the next year, the words you hear all around you are, "Merry Christmas, see you next year!"

Everyone leaves with a smile on their face and the true meaning of Christmas in their hearts!

William and Mary's Yule Log

UST IMAGINE SOME STUDENTS dressed up in yeoman costumes and administrators and faculty members in colonial coats, waistcoats, and breeches, their wives in elaborate silk and brocade gowns, all participating in a grand Christmas party.

That was the case on December 20, 1934, when the new president of the College of William and Mary in Williamsburg, Virginia, declared "a revival of ancient customs" at the school chartered in 1693. John Stewart Bryan wanted to bring old English customs back to the old "English" school.

To kick off the celebration, costumed freshmen, looking much like merry men from a Robin Hood movie, with great flair and much pomp, marched into the Great Hall of the Sir Christopher Wren Building carrying a large Yule Log on their shoulders. Into the grand fireplace of the hall the log was carefully placed and lit.

Their fellow students then passed through the hall, picking up sprigs of holly at the doorway, and individually tossed the greens on the flaming log. Traditions have it that one either was casting off old worries or wishing for good luck in the new year.

A host of other activities were encompassed within the Christmas party festivities provided by President Bryan at no cost to the college. It would be, however, the Yule Log ceremony that would become the major holiday tradition at William and Mary that continues to this day – about three-quarters of a century later.

In colonial times – both in Virginia and in England – many a great log was burned and many a drink was quaffed beside ample hearths as revelers observed the Yule Log ceremony.

Today, several centuries later, in addition to the college ceremony, many people still enjoy the festivities and delight in the merriment associated with one of the oldest English holiday customs.

In many homes throughout Virginia – from the sands of the Chesapeake to the mountains of the Blue Ridge – the burning of the log is still a much-awaited event, frequently as part of Christmas Eve plans. Some towns and cities in Virginia, such as Chatham and Norfolk, have maintained Yule Log celebrations, while many of William and Mary's local alumni chapters re-create the event of their college days.

Yule Log blessings also have been passed down through the years:

> May this fire burn brightly, so that its light will seek out and
> bring happiness to those less fortunate than we, and bring
> peace on earth, good will to men.

As the log burns, wine is sprinkled on it and another chant is offered: "Burn the log, o fire! Fire! Burn away all evil!"

It is believed that the Yule Log ceremony became a part of the English Christmas festival through the Vikings, who, at their feast of juul at the winter solstice, kindled bonfires of huge logs in honor of their god Thor.

It is not known when men first used fire in worship and celebrations of joyous occasions, but historians say the Egyptians and Persians used fire in religious services centuries before the time of Christ.

Later, in medieval times in England, a whole tree trunk was placed in the fireplace of the baronial hall. The tradition came to America with the first settlements of Englishmen in the early 17th century. However, the lonely, dreary days and problems of the settlements, especially at Jamestown, delayed the merry festivities for probably at least a decade.

Scattered 18th-century records indicate that the Yule Log tradition was well kept by Virginia planters along the James River. In preparation for the celebration, an oak, pine, or ash tree was felled, cut, marked, and hidden away in the forest.

At the appropriate time, the field hands and household servants went out in search of it and dragged the log to the main house. There it was split in half – one part going on the fire and the other saved for use in kindling the fire the following year.

Many superstitions grew up around the Yule Log. It was considered bad luck if it did not burn for the full 12 days of Christmas, which began on Christmas Eve and lasted until dusk on January 6.

Servants watered the log down at the day's end to preserve it through the holiday season since many planters excused their servants from all their duties as long as the log burned.

In another practice, the ashes from the log were diluted with water and swallowed as a cure for internal disorders. They also were made into a paste and applied externally for infections.

The Virginia Almanack of 1711 expressed a Christmas wish, which was probably repeated during many Yule Log ceremonies in Virginia that winter:

We wish you health, and good fires, diversion, and good company; honest trading, and good success; loving courtship and good wives; and lastly, merry Christmas and a happy new year.

❄   ❄   ❄

ALONG WITH THE YULE LOG, several other English traditions have become part of our Christmas celebration.

"Here we come a wassailing, among the leaves so green!" is the beginning of a holiday carol that expresses that the carolers feel "Love and joy come to you, And to you your wassail too, And God bless you and send you a happy New Year, and God send you a happy new year."

Wassailing, a very ancient custom, is simply going door-to-door singing carols to your friends. The word *wassail* comes from the Anglo-Saxon phrase "Waes Hael" – meaning good health. To help the happiness along, the wassail also was a drink served for the carolers. Initially, it was a mixture of curdled cream, roasted apples, eggs, cloves, nutmeg, sugar, ginger, and mulled ale, served in a large bowl – the wassail bowl.

Early on the festivities were enjoyed on New Year's Eve and Twelfth Night. Later, however, wassailing was performed "and drunk" anytime during the holiday season.

❄   ❄   ❄

CHRISTMAS CRACKERS became part of the English Christmas in the late 1840s when Thomas Smith took a French concept of wrapping a bon-bon in tissue paper and twisting both ends. Smith put other sweets in his paper and eventually used a cardboard tube and filled it with a variety of goodies.

Later he added a piece of chemically treated paper that when pulled created a "pop:" hence the "cracker" was born. The brightly colored paper crackers now often contain a party hat, a balloon, a small piece of paper with a corny joke printed on it, and a small gift.

Crackers are used to decorate the Christmas table and are pulled before the meal begins. The hats are put on and the very corny jokes read. Then the dinner can be served.

❋   ❋   ❋

ANOTHER WONDERFUL English Christmas practice was the celebrated Christmas pudding. It originated in England, probably in medieval times, but no one really knows when. Early on it was called either "figgy" pudding or plum pudding and was originally a spiced porridge.

It became an official part of the English Christmas dinner ritual when Prince Albert of Saxe-Gotha, Prince Consort of Queen Victoria of England, introduced it to his family and friends.

Traditionally, the puddings are made about five weeks before Christmas and begun on "Stir-up Sunday" – that falls directly before the beginning of Advent. The plum pudding is a "very rich, dark pudding made with all sorts of dried fruits, nuts, spices, black treacle and lots of sherry or brandy." They are steamed when first made, and then re-steamed on Christmas Day before being served with a white sauce or brandy butter.

There is a custom that some people hide a coin or trinket in the pudding and the person who finds the surprise will get good luck in the coming year and their "pudding wish, made when the pudding was being prepared, will come true!"

JEANNE NICHOLSON SILER

101 Roanoke Stars

LIKE ALL GOOD CHRISTMAS SEASONS, the story of the Roanoke stars began in November. November 23, to be precise, on Thanksgiving Eve in 1949.

Today, most Virginians know of the one big star that gives this mid-sized city its nickname, "Star City of the South." Illuminated by 2,000 feet of neon tubing, the massive star is not only the property of the city of Roanoke, it's also a beloved landmark and a nightlight for thousands.

But in the beginning, there were lots of Roanoke stars.

In 1949, the Roanoke Merchants Association dreamed up the concept of decorating the city's downtown streets for the coming Christmas season with a hundred neon stars. A membership drive also raised funds to put up a matching oversized star on Mill Mountain, which overlooks the metropolitan area.

On the 23rd, the so-called "baby" stars were ready. Hanging along Campbell and Church avenues and on Jefferson Street, they drew crowds of residents downtown for the start of the holiday season. Everyone was eager to see the new illuminated decorations, manufactured by the local Roy C.

Kinsey Sign Company. Seventy-five Boy Scouts did the honors and switched them on.

While the lights were being lit downtown, choirs, color guards, and congressmen gathered on the mountaintop for official ceremonies. Roanoke native and former U.S. Rep. Clifton A. Woodrum, speaking atop Mill Mountain that night, praised the giant 88.5-foot star (the frame is 100 feet in height) as a symbol.

"As the Star of Bethlehem guided the wise men of old to a place of peace and tranquility," Woodrum said, "so the wise men of Roanoke and neighboring cities and counties will be guided to this, 'The City of the Star,' where they will find a hearty welcome in true southern fashion," he continued, according to *Roanoke Times* archives.

Also on hand for the star lighting was Roanoke native John Payne – at that time a leading man in Hollywood films. In fact, just two years earlier Payne had starred in the original "Miracle on 34th Street," now a wonderful Christmas film classic. Payne portrayed attorney Fred Gailey, who defended Kris Kringle in his claim to be the real Santa Claus.

When the star was lit, traffic in downtown Roanoke, below the mountain, came to a standstill, according to newspaper accounts. On Brandon Avenue, cars were bumper-to-bumper for half a mile. Arthur Robertson, an Eastern Airlines pilot in a plane above the city, reported, "It's the most beautiful thing I've ever seen."

Three Kinsey sons – Warren, Bob, and Roy Jr. – worked in their father's sign company, which contracted to design, fabricate, and install the big Mill Mountain star. Several years ago, Roy, Jr. recalled that the scariest part of the construction was tieing neon onto the star points. It was the star, the installers, and then "nothing but the sky beyond," he said. Over the next 60 years the Kinsey family never tried "to cash in on [the star]. We never had our name on it," brother Bob added. "We just built the stars as Christmas decorations."

In 2013, brother Bob tried to set the record straight regarding who came up with the Roanoke star concept. "The idea was my father's who sold it to the merchants association and the chamber of commerce. We had no idea that the public would fall in love with the big star. Some of the city officials and the editor of the local newspaper just thought it was a tacky neon sign, but the citizens didn't want it to go away."

The city of Roanoke has continuously maintained the star. It was refurbished in 1999 for its 50th anniversary at a cost of $60,000, more than double the $27,000 cost of the original project.

Both the large star and the smaller three-foot stars were initially used just on the nights between Thanksgiving and New Year's, the smaller ones giving shoppers of all ages a special treat during the 1950s and '60s. Going downtown was a "vital" part of the holiday season, according to Jim Crawford, who grew up, as he puts it, on "the dark side of the star." (Garden City residents who, like the rest of the city's citizens, had joyfully anticipated the lighting of the large star that night in 1949, were crushed to realize the neon lights were only visible on the north-facing side of the structure.)

As memorable as the little three-foot neon stars were, they were eventually taken out of service by the city. They may have been deemed outdated or too difficult to maintain, but by 1972, only 23 of the original 100 were still in working order. These were sold to the nearby town of Floyd for $20 apiece.

The stars then brightened the holiday streets of Floyd for another decade and a half. But by the 1980s, someone decided the little Kinsey neon stars needed replacing again. This time, they were abandoned on a piece of town property, left on the hillside as scrap.

A baby star, circa 1953, at the corner of Campbell Avenue and Jefferson Street

That is, until Richard Lewis, Floyd's town manager at the time, came to the rescue. And that's when a second Christmas star story was born.

Lewis knew that his wife, Megan McKewan, an artist, liked interesting art objects – including neon. Lewis also knew where the little stars had been discarded, so he salvaged the one still-working star and refurbished it for Megan as a Christmas present. It hung in their living room for a number of years; then, before she retired, it moved outdoors to a spot where she could see its blue glow during her commute home.

"We live very rurally," said McKewan, "The driveway is probably a half mile long, and Rick would turn the star on in the evening so I could see it when I rounded one of the last curves." These days, the star hangs in her studio. She plugs in it for parties, book club meetings, or "just whenever I feel like it."

The story of salvation continues, however.

In 2009, in conjunction with the publicity surrounding the 60th anniversary of the big star on Mill Mountain, the junked little stars were rediscovered. Though the original neon tubing was broken, the star-shaped metal frames were in good shape. According to Karen Hodges, Floyd clerk and treasurer, because of all the local fascination, "we sent our guys up on the hill and drug 'em all out and cleaned them up. Sort of."

Hodges recalls there was so much sentimental interest in the little stars that Floyd resorted to holding an auction the following summer, during the annual June Jubilee. "We must have had 150 people come out," she remembers. "We had [the stars] on a flat-bed trailer and used an old-time auctioneer."

The town sold 20 stars at prices that ranged from $50 to $200, with Kinsey family descendants winning the bid on at least four of them. "We made a big deal out of their whole [Kinsey] family coming up from Roanoke as the stars' original designers. We had seats of honor for them," says Hodges.

Another interested party was Virginia Museum of Transportation Executive Director Bev Fitzpatrick, who had learned of Floyd's plan to auction off the baby star remnants, and had inquired about receiving one for the museum. The town of Floyd kept one, and made a gift of another for the museum – so, counting McKewan's, all 23 were accounted for.

And thus it was that one little star made its way back to Roanoke.

Fitzpatrick saw to it that, carefully restored with new neon tubes by Budget Signs of Roanoke, the 60-plus-year-old star was hung in the Roanoke museum's Automobile Gallery, casting its soft glow once more on Fords, Chevrolets, and Studebakers – just as it would have on Campbell Avenue or Jefferson Street in 1949.

"I was born in Roanoke," says Fitzpatrick, who is only a little older than the star in his museum, "and as a child I

Campbell Avenue's light poles are decorated with baby stars, circa 1950.

remember the little stars. They were everywhere. They were all different colors: white, green, yellow. ... We're thrilled to have one. Ours is baby blue and it looks really cool."

Floyd's current town manager, Lance Terpenny, notes that the town council chose not only to keep one of the original three-foot stars for display in their council chambers during the holidays, but also recently commissioned four new half-size neon stars – yellow, red, blue, and green – to go with the original. Proving too fragile to hang outdoors, all five are now displayed in council chambers.

Meanwhile, the magic of Roanoke's Mill Mountain star continues to awe area residents year-round.

When city officials realized the immense popularity of the star during the holidays, they decided it should shine brightly every night. In 1976, the color changed from white to red, white, and blue to commemorate the nation's bicentennial. It went back to white, but was changed again to the three-color patriotic theme after the 9-11 terrorist attack in New York City and Washington. In 2007, the star's glow returned to all-white as a sign of hope following the Virginia Tech shootings. The red, white, and blue colors are now be displayed annually only on patriotic holidays.

The star has always held a special place in the hearts of citizens.

Jim Crawford, a Roanoke filmmaker, proposed to his wife, Cathy, under the star. Crawford's brother and sister-in-law, like many before them, chose to get married under it: Dan Crawford and Mary Bishop tied the knot in 1998 – just a few weeks before Christmas. Bishop remembers it was a warm day for December, and there were just four of them: the husband-and wife-to-be, the minister, and a photographer. And the view, of course.

"We mostly walk our dog up there now, but the view, looking out to the Allegheny mountains and over the Roanoke Valley that we live in ... it's fantastic, really," Bishop declares. "It costs nothing to go up there, and we like it how it is such a unifier for the city.

"We take visitors up the mountain, and when we get to the overlook we always hear other languages, which is such a neat thing. There are people from all over the world there, snapping pictures."

The Star of the South shines each evening from dark until midnight – with a little extra sparkle, of course, during the Christmas season.

What About Eggnog?

WHAT IS IT ABOUT EGGNOG? That delicious beaten egg, sweet cream, and liquor concoction probably was first created in the 17th century in England and came to this country in the 18th century through its ruling aristocracy – the planters in colonial America – who made the drink a part of their Christmas holiday festivities.

It's easy to see where the *egg* in eggnog comes from. But what about the *nog*? Some historians or linguists believe *nog* refers to *noggin*, a small wooden mug for beer. In East Anglia, the area between Ipswich and Norwich in England, *nog* shows up in the late 17th century as a regional term for a strong beer. It was described as such by Humphrey Prideaux in a 1693 letter written from the county of Norfolk, England.

John F. Mariani, in *The Dictionary of American Food and Drink*, said the word *eggnog* did not appear in print in America until the publishing of a broadside in 1775. He noted that the British ale and wine had been replaced by rum and American whiskey.

In Colonial America, rum was commonly called "grog." Therefore, it is quite possible that the drink was called, "egg-and-grog," which, when modified or corrupted, could become "eggnog."

However, there is still another idea. Maybe the "egg-and-grog" was combined with the container to become "egg and grog in a noggin."

Could that be shortened to "eggnog"? Who knows!

Ben Zimmer, a language columnist for the *Boston Globe* and former columnist of *The New York Times Magazine*, did much research on the origin of eggnog. He found another published mention in the March 26, 1788, edition of the *New-Jersey Journal*. It reported:

> *A young man with a cormorant appetite, voraciously*
> *devoured, last week, at Connecticut farms, thirty raw eggs,*
> *a glass of egg nog, and another of brandy sling.*

About six months later a Philadelphia newspaper reported alcoholic indigestion "when wine and beer, punch and eggnog meet, instantly ensues a quarrel."

A Norfolk, Virginia newspaper — the *Virginia Chronicle* — reported in January 1793 one of the first instances where eggnog was part of Christmas merriment. Linguistics scholar Joel S. Berson found this reference:

> *On last Christmas Eve several gentlemen met at Northampton*
> *Court-house, and spent the evening in mirth and festivity,*
> *when EGG-NOG was the principal Liquor used by the*
> *company. After they had indulged pretty freely in this beverage,*
> *a gentleman in the company offered a bet that not one of*
> *the party could write four verses, extempore, which should be*
> *rhyme and sense...*

In response, one of the revelers wrote in part:

> *'Tis Egg-Nog now whose golden streams dispense*

Far richer treasurers to the ravish'd sense.
The Muse from Wine derives a transient glare,
But Egg-Nog's draughts afford her solid fare.

Zimmer reported all of these references to eggnog, but in a kind of throwaway paragraph mentions that "there's also a recipe floating around that is supposedly from the 'kitchen papers' of George Washington at Mount Vernon. I have no idea if it's legitimate," he wrote.

A check of the *Papers of George Washington*, a multivolume chronicle, reveals no mention of "eggnog." The estate of Mount Vernon, operated today as a historic site, makes no mention of such a recipe. There are, however, many accounts in 20th-century magazines and newspapers that recount stories of Washington offering eggnog to his many guests during the holidays at Mount Vernon. So, the Washington egg recipe stuck.

One such account says that Washington, who enjoyed strong drink all his life, incorporated brandy, whiskey, sherry, and Jamaica rum in his mixture. It is said that there was no mention of how many eggs to use in the recipe.

Washington's eggnog recipe, modified for today's use, calls for:

One pint of brandy	30 eggs
Half-pint of rye whiskey	12 tablespoons sugar
Quarter-pint of Jamaica rum	One quart of milk
Quarter-pint of sherry	One quart of whipping cream, whipped

The liquor should be mixed first. Separate eggs. Beat yolks, add sugar. Mix well. Add liquor mixture slowly, beating constantly. Add milk, then whipped cream while slowly beating. Beat egg whites until stiff and fold slowly into mixture. Allow to stand in a cool place for several days. "Taste frequently," the recipe concluded.

This version of Washington's eggnog serves about 50 persons, like other early recipes that made large quantities.

Eggnog made its way into the history of West Point, the nation's military academy when, in 1826, young cadets decided to violate the no-alcohol rule and celebrate Christmas by making eggnog, a tradition believed to have been passed down from General Washington. Again, there is no documentation of such a practice.

The West Point party was planned secretly and successfully held, but it was the after-effects that caused the problem. The cadets – intoxicated – got somewhat out of hand, resulting in the so-called "Eggnog Riot," involving at least 70 cadets, 20 of whom were court-martialed. Ten of the young men were expelled, and several more resigned.

Several years later, with no references to military use, cookbook author Elizabeth Leslie, in her 1851 edition of *Directions for Cookery*, wrote the first published account of an eggnog recipe:

> Beat separately the yolks and whites of six eggs. Stir the yolks into a quart of rich milk, or thin cream, add half a pound of sugar. Then mix in half a pint of rum or brandy. Flavor with grated nutmeg. Lastly, stir in gently the beaten whites of three eggs. It should be mixed in a china bowl.

Another Virginian, credited in various publications as being an eggnog specialist, was Mary Anna Custis Lee, wife of General Robert E. Lee. Again, Mrs. Lee's eggnog recipe has become another long-lasting tale. One such account for Mrs. Lee's eggnog mixture is *The Robert E. Lee Family Cooking and*

Housekeeping Book, written in 2002 by Anne Carter Zimmer, their great-granddaughter.

A careful examination of the book, however, reveals that it was not Mary Lee, but rather Jennie Letcher, wife of Virginia's Civil War governor, whose eggnog recipe is cited. Mrs. Lee, on several occasions, Zimmer writes, enjoyed Mrs. Letcher's "spirited" eggnog, which required only brandy and rum and ten eggs to make four or five quarts. The blend should be allowed to "ripen" in a cold but not freezing place. An unheated room or porch did fine for Jennie Letcher.

An English visitor to America remarked in 1866,

> Christmas is not properly observed unless you brew egg nogg for all comers; everybody calls on everybody else; and each call is celebrated with a solemn egg-nogging... It is made cold and is drunk cold and is to be commended.

These days, few people make their eggnog from "scratch." Rather, they buy it already prepared in quart or half-gallon containers at the grocery store. All that is left is the blending in of the liquor.

So, here's to Mrs. Lee and General Washington. Cheers!

he stable. At night more than 50,000 lights reflected in the
morial garden where the Nativity was assembled.

Coleman's was open at no charge to the visitors. "We've
ays wanted to do something for the community," Morgan
. "It's not only good for other people, but also builds better
ness for us later."

Indeed, that was the case for my family. More than 20 years
that first visit, I returned with my two young sons, Walker
Carter. Like their older sister, the boys were immediately
ivated by the holiday dream world. In 2001, the magical
t was still there with hundreds more moving figures and
ably a half million sparkling lights.

For the boys, however, it was Santa's Circus with all the
ns and Santa's Train that quickly became favorites. They just
I and marveled at the scenes – all the motion, color, and
. Even though the family walked through many other scenes
nter snow with cavorting bears, a toy factory, and others, the
ers wanted to go back to see the train and circus.

They also enjoyed some new scenes that had appeared over
ears, like the Penguin Construction Company, the Bear Sled
ry, and the amazing Beaver Log Camp.

Two years later, in 2003, Coleman's Nursery faced a
ing decision. The City of Portsmouth and the YMCA of
mouth wanted their property for a new library and an
ded YMCA. What to do? Nursery owners Twiford and
n were getting older and felt the time had come to close
an's. But what about the "Christmas Wonderland? What
be done to save this annual treat?

he Portsmouth Museums Foundation came to the rescue
ecided to raise the $175,000 needed to purchase the
and all the related props of the community tradition.
wiford, then 75 years old, was excited when the purchase
came a reality with an announcement to the community

Coleman's
Christmas Wonderland

B Y THE TIME my family had the opportunity to
visit "Christmas Wonderland" at Coleman's Nursery in 1980, the holiday spectacle was already a South
Hampton Roads tradition. For thousands of people, it had become
an important part of their Christmas season – something not to
be missed!

As a newspaper bureau chief, I had heard about Coleman's
in the Churchland section of Portsmouth, but never took the
time to visit until I found myself looking for a "great Christmas story" that could be published during Christmas week in
December 1980. What I discovered, and tried to convey to my
readers, was an absolute fairyland.

There were thousands of colored lights and several hundred animated figures – bears, penguins, angels, elves, toy
soldiers – and a host of mechanical displays. Model trains, a
circus sideshow, flying stars, and dozens of other figures were
arranged in various scenes of splendid animation.

On that first visit, my photographer and I were greeted by

one of the nursery owners, Floyd Twiford, who couldn't wait to show us around the various Christmas scenes that had been created by his employees.

That late-afternoon experience, which took on a more exciting glow with nightfall, was such an amazing adventure that several days later I brought my then nearly five-year-old daughter, Anne-Evan, to see all the magic.

And what a treat it turned out to be. Her eyes grew big and bright as she walked through room after room of lights and animated figures. She stood in amazement, not wanting to move to another scene. Each elaborately decorated room with starry skies and billowing balls of cotton told a different story and took her on a different Christmas holiday journey.

Through the next years, Anne-Evan wanted to share her wonderful holiday treat with her friends and playmates. We would drive to Portsmouth and visit the nursery for several hours. Through the years, Megan, Evan, and Jennifer all enjoyed our Coleman's Nursery adventure at least once or maybe twice. Coming home we sometimes sang carols, but more often the kids just yakked about the Wonderland.

Every holiday season from 1966 through 2003, Coleman's Nursery personnel transformed various sections of the nursery – storage areas for seed and fertilizer and sections for spring and summer bedding plants – into a world the Christmas Wonderland of brightly colored lights with wonderful holiday music played through hidden speakers.

So popular was Coleman's that hundreds of visitors would stand in line just to enter the nursery, and frequently stand in another line to visit one of their favorite scenes.

Luring visitors, like my daughter, were sections of the Wonderland titled Babes in Iceland, Wonderland Forest, and Candyland. A large separate building in the rear of the nursery was called The Ice Palace and featured displays such as

Christmas of 1890, Santa's Workshop, and S

This holiday extravaganza began in 1 "Junie" Lancaster, then owner of Coleman's a World's Fair exhibit in New York. Lanc employee Twiford, and original owner Jc Pepsi-Cola exhibit with animated figures. something like that would work during nursery.

The Wonderland began with the pur ure – a sleeping Santa Claus that seemingly his bed until Christmas Eve. The followin figures were added, and soon the elabo develop.

Twiford and another employee, Dal Coleman's in early 1980 and expanded further. "This just didn't come together den," Morgan told me on my first visit. little each year. The new figures are son scenes or merely added to enrich old fav

The job of putting the holiday c not an easy one, Twiford said. It rout weeks prior to Thanksgiving to transfo holiday delight. "Near Thanksgiving finish, we easily worked 12 to 18 hou created," Twiford explained.

Morgan added that every nursery holiday scenes, with more than 600 the project. Lots of cotton was hung with flocking and crystal flakes on the images.

By 1980, more than 200 mechan with hundreds of thousands of minia was a near-life-size Nativity scene,

A Victorian ice-skating scene from Coleman's Christmas Wonderland.

on December 19, 2003. "This is a real Christmas present for me," he said. "The best one it could possibly be. I can't begin to tell you how happy I am about it."

Thus, January 4, 2004, was the final day for the Christmas Wonderland at Coleman's Nursery and the tradition continued. But a new tradition began later that year on Thanksgiving Day, when the Courthouse Galleries in the old 1846 courthouse on Portsmouth's High Street opened for the holidays. The Galleries (later renamed the Portsmouth Art & Cultural Center) were transformed into the new venue for Coleman's treats, and "Winter Wonderland" was officially reborn.

The Foundation set about restoring and upgrading the animated figures and various pieces of background art that comprised the scenes. The Coleman collection was so large that not every scene could be displayed in its new quarters; therefore, each year's exhibits contain some old favorites, while newer ones are added.

Every year families return to see their favorite Coleman scenes at Portsmouth's High Street art center, while newcomers, just learning of the tradition, get an opportunity to add the experience to their own Christmas traditions.

JAMES A. MCMAHON

Tangier Island Holly Run

TANGIER ISLAND, ABOUT 12 MILES off the Eastern Shore in the Chesapeake Bay, just south of the Maryland-Virginia line, was discovered by Captain John Smith in 1608 and so named because it reminded him of that island off the coast of Africa. But as with so many facts about the Eastern Shore, there is even dispute about this naming. Historians now believe Smith called Tangier and other nearby islands "Russell Isles" for a Doctor Russell who was aboard his ship.

Smith's records indicate that the island was covered in pine trees and green even in winter, but time and strong storms have eliminated the greenery and the island is bare and brown in the winter. That was the way it looked when Ed Nabb of Cambridge, Maryland, landed his green and white 1946 Ercoupe on the island in the winter of 1968.

For years the only way to get to Tangier was by boat. Everything was brought in by boat, but that changed, too, in 1967. A runway was constructed by the Federal Government as an emergency landing strip for the Patuxent Naval Air Station. Small general aviation aircraft were banned from using the strip but they managed to sneak in anyway. At least that's how local lore has it.

In fact, if you talk to the pilots at Patuxent they just laugh at the thought of it being their emergency strip because they know of no aircraft flying from their base that could land at Tangier. As it turns out, the runway was constructed by the Virginia Department of Aviation for the use of small general aviation aircraft.

During Nabb's visit to his favorite Tangier sandwich shop he talked "with my daughter, Lorraine, who at the time worked as a waitress in a local restaurant," explained Virginia Marshall, a Tangier native. "When he walked around, he saw that we had no holly trees. From then on, he would fly here, always on a Saturday or Sunday, depending on the weather, to bring holly to us before Christmas."

The first Holly Run was in December 1968 when Nabb arrived with two bags of holly; he gave one to the Swain Memorial United Methodist Church and the other to the New

Holly Run plane approaches tiny Tangier Island

Testament Church. But a problem arose over the lack of support in the Bible for decorating the church. It was clearly a pagan custom and it gave the church fathers some pause.

After discussions, however, it was decided that the spirit of the gesture should be the guiding force and the holly was accepted. "After receiving the holly," Mrs. Marshall explained, "we would take it and drape it around the altar in the church, but the children would take the berries off when they were having their Christmas program. They would become distracted and forget their lines. So now we place the holly in the church windows and in two white urns outside the church."

In the ensuing years word spread among the pilot communities around the Chesapeake and the one-man show started to look more like a small squadron of little planes. The Tangier Island Holly Run was born.

By 1975, seven planes carrying the big plastic bags full of holly arrived on the island and with them, for the first time, was Santa Claus in the form of Mike A. Wingo, a Cambridge radio announcer. The current Santa is James Schultz of Ocean City, Maryland. Jim is Santa and needs no props or costumes to achieve his magic. Jim volunteered for the job on the condition that he be allowed to buy presents for the children out of his own pocket. The toys he brings are carefully selected and treasured by the children.

As the years have gone by the size of the group has grown and in one year 45 planes made the trip to Tangier. Originally the trip began at Ed Nabb Sr.'s home airport – Cambridge-Dorchester Airport; it originates now at the Bay Bridge Airport in Stevensville, Maryland. It is scheduled for the first Saturday in December with the following Saturday to be used if the weather is bad. Dozens of pilots fly in early for coffee and donuts and to renew old friendships. In the past, the mayor of Cambridge would address the group, welcoming them to Cambridge and providing a short synopsis of the day's schedule.

Then Ed Nabb would address the group, giving a short history of the Holly Run, and would explain the departure sequence: "First the slower planes will depart, and then the faster ones and the faster ones will pass the slower ones and land first. We'll put Santa Claus in one of the faster planes so he can get to Tangier first." The takeoff can take a while because of the sheer number of planes involved, but fortunately, there has never been an accident or incident associated with the Holly Run.

After all the planes arrive on Tangier and are tied down, Virginia Marshall greets the group (as she has done nearly every year since the first holly run) along with Hattie Bowden. All the holly in large green bags is loaded onto golf carts (the primary

locomotive transportation on the island) with Santa and his gigantic bag also in a golf cart for the short trip to the community room at the church where all the young children of the island are waiting.

The looks on those children's faces as Santa comes through the door is something to behold and has moved more

Bags of holly for Tangier Island

than one pilot to say what an excellent way to start the holiday season! After Santa hands out the presents and some refreshments are had, the pilots wend their way to the Swain Methodist Church for what, for many of us, is the best part of the trip – a discussion of life on Tangier Island led by Virginia Marshall and several of her friends.

Most of the pilots know the short version of the history of Tangier. After its discovery in 1608 not much happened. It was the summer retreat for the little-known Pocomoke Indians; their existence is documented by the thousands of stone arrowheads that have been found. Some say the island was purchased from the Indians in 1666 by a Mr. West from the mainland for "two overcoats." Again, it's island lore. However, John West of Maryland ultimately did receive a patent for islands in the Chesapeake about 10 years later. Tradition says the West land was sold to a John Crockett, maybe an ancestor of Davy Crockett of Tennessee, who settled the island with his eight sons in 1686. No records, however, survive. But by 1900 the population was nearly 1,200, one-third of whom were Crocketts.

The island gained some fame during the War of 1812 when it served as a British naval base. The islanders were mostly Tories and were hospitable to the soldiers who took some pains to not offend or abuse them. The older people can remember their great-grandparents telling of the soldiers walking single-file through the corn to reach the well. They avoided damaging the corn. Prior to their departure for the attack on Fort McHenry outside Baltimore (where the words to the "Star Spangled Banner" were written), the soldiers received a strong sermon from a native preacher named Joshua Thomas (Mrs. Marshall's great-grandfather). He is said to have forecast their defeat at Fort McHenry.

There has never been any established industry on the island; most of the population makes a living from the waters of the Chesapeake Bay. As the quality and quantity of oysters and crabs has declined in the Bay, so too has the Tangier population; there are only 600 today. Also in decline is the size of the island as the waters of the Chesapeake rise. Some estimates put the loss at about 25 feet a year on the western part of the island. With the decline in fishing, some islanders have turned to the tourist industry that is fed by daily boat service from Crisfield, Maryland and Reedville, Virginia.

This is the background against which the pilots assemble in

the Swain Methodist Church every December to hear how the people are coping with these difficult issues which come on top of the challenges of living in an isolated community.

The man who started the Holly Run, Ed Nabb Sr., was very much a product of what Tom Brokaw called "The Greatest Generation." Ed, a practicing attorney, never went to college. After serving in the Army in both World War II and Korea, he returned to Cambridge, Maryland, and read law in an office the old fashioned way – the way Abe Lincoln did. Although known mostly as a prominent Cambridge attorney, he was better known as a fearless speedboat racer and aircraft pilot.

He also wrote articles on marine engines for several boating magazines from the 1940s to the 1970s. He was elected to the Marine Racing Hall of Fame in 1947. Ed was president of the Nathan Foundation for more than 20 years and gave more than $700,000 in scholarships during that time.

Ed was known as a great storyteller, "a good old Eastern Shore boy," as one of his friends put it. He was passionate about preserving the Eastern Shore's history for all. He would say, "Let's face it, the Chesapeake Bay region is where the United States began and there should be a repository here for that information."

Ed believed in giving his money away while he was still alive. To that end, he endowed a research center at Salisbury University in the sum of $500,000, now called the Edward H. Nabb Research Center for Delmarva History and Culture. The Center has many invaluable historical documents and oral histories of the old days on the Eastern Shore.

Ed Nabb died on June 2, 2002, but for Tangier Island, his legacy lives on with the annual Holly Run and an exhibit in the island's history museum.

MISCELLANY

Yes, Virginia,
There *is* a Santa Claus

I N THE LATE SUMMER OF 1897, Virginia O'Hanlon asked her father, Dr. Philip O'Hanlon, who was also New York coroner's assistant, if there really was a Santa Claus. He responded simply, "If you see it in *The Sun*, it's so."

Virginia sat down and wrote to *The Sun*, which was, at the time, a prominent New York City newspaper along with *The New York Times* and *The New York Herald*. On September 21, 1897, *The Sun*'s response appeared written by Francis Pharcellus Church, lead editorial writer of his brother's newspaper. It did not become known until after his death in 1906 that he was the author of the Santa Claus editorial.

Church's reply, printed on the newspaper's front page, has become legendary, in part for its philosophical tone and its forthright treatment. It is now a major part of American Christmas lore, as follows:

IS THERE A SANTA CLAUS?

We take pleasure in answering at once and thus prominently

the communication below, expressing at the same time our great gratification that its faithful author is numbered among the friends of THE SUN:

DEAR EDITOR: I am 8 years old. Some of my little friends say there is no Santa Claus. Papa says, "If you see it in THE SUN it's so." Please tell me the truth; is there a Santa Claus?
VIRGINIA O'HANLON.
115 WEST NINETY-FIFTH STREET.

VIRGINIA, your little friends are wrong. They have been affected by the skepticism of a skeptical age. They do not believe except [what] they see. They think that nothing can be which is not comprehensible by their little minds. All minds, Virginia, whether they be men's or children's, are little. In this great universe of ours, man is a mere insect, an ant, in his intellect, as compared with the boundless world about him, as measured by the intelligence capable of grasping the whole of truth and knowledge.

Yes, VIRGINIA, there is a Santa Claus. He exists as certainly as love and generosity and devotion exist, and you know that they abound and give to your life its highest beauty and joy. Alas! How dreary would be the world if there were no Santa Claus. It would be as dreary as if there were no VIRGINIAs. There would be no childlike faith then, no poetry, no romance to make tolerable this existence. We should have no enjoyment, except in sense and sight. The eternal light with which childhood fills the world would be extinguished.

Not believe in Santa Claus! You might as well not believe in fairies! You might get your papa to hire men to watch in all the chimneys on Christmas Eve to catch Santa Claus, but even if they did not see Santa Claus coming down, what would that prove? Nobody sees Santa Claus, but that is no sign that there is no Santa Claus. The most real things in the world are those that neither children nor men can see. Did you ever see fairies dancing on the lawn? Of course not, but that's no proof that they are not there. Nobody can conceive or imagine all the wonders there are unseen and unseeable in the world.

You may tear apart the baby's rattle and see what makes the noise inside, but there is a veil covering the unseen world which not the strongest man, nor even the united strength of all the strongest men that ever lived, could tear apart. Only faith, fancy, poetry, love, romance, can push aside that curtain and view and picture the supernal beauty and glory beyond. Is it all real? Ah, VIRGINIA, in all this world there is nothing else real and abiding.

No Santa Claus! Thank God! He lives, and he lives forever. A thousand years from now, Virginia, nay, ten times ten thousand years from now, he will continue to make glad the heart of childhood.

❄   ❄   ❄

LAURA VIRGINIA O'HANLON was born in New York City on July 20, 1889. She graduated from Hunter College in 1910; received her master's degree from Columbia University in 1912; and earned her doctorate from Fordham University. Her professional career was spent as an educator; she retired in 1959. Throughout her career she was asked about her letter and often she replied, "All I did was ask the question: I did not do anything special. Of course, Mr. Church's editorial was so beautiful [that] everyone remembers his words. It was Mr. Church who did something wonderful." She died in 1971.

ANNE-EVAN WILLIAMS

A Sleigh Full of Cards

IT SEEMS THAT EVERYONE who celebrates Christmas has a different way of enjoying the annual barrage of Christmas cards. Growing up, our household had a small wooden sleigh, just the right size for holding a collection of Christmas cards. How I loved watching them arrive – glittering Madonnas, snowy cardinals, Christmas trees, and Santas, all adorning cards with warm sentiments from friends and family! I eagerly awaited the arrival of the card from a dear family friend, whose card every year included a homemade ornament for our tree! I was allowed to open the cards as they arrived, and place them carefully into the card sleigh, where they remained for the holiday season.

When I was married, I watched my mother-in-law display them differently. She hung them carefully around the kitchen doorway, displaying each one proudly for all the family to enjoy. By the time Christmas arrived, the doorway leading to the heart of the home was completely framed with thoughtful words from loved ones.

Even my grandmother had her own unique way of display-ing her cards. She mounted them to an antique room screen, and sometimes left them there for the better part of the year.

Yet another friend has a plain wreath of greenery in her foyer. Her Christmas cards get tucked carefully into the wreath as they arrive; by the end of Advent, her Christmas card wreath is fully decorated with images of the holiday season and words of love. It's hard to imagine Christmas is truly approaching without the arrival of these cards in the mail.

Yet Christmas cards are a relatively new part of our holiday traditions. The tradition that now seems such an integral part of our Christmas preparations began in 1843, when Sir Henry Cole in London commissioned an illustration from John Callcott Horsley, with the simple greeting, "A Merry Christmas and A Happy New Year to You."

Throughout the years Cole had made it a practice to send short notes to his friends at Christmas, wishing them a happy holiday and good fortune for the coming year. However, in 1843 he found himself too busy for such notes and commissioned a friend, Horsley, to design a card, which would replace his personal notes.

The card featured an elaborate design, divided into three panels with the primary center sketch in color, showing a festive party scene with the group raising their wine glasses in a toast. On either side of the card were panels representing two of the holiday's oldest traditions – clothing the needy and feeding the hungry.

While the greeting was simple and to-the-point, it served as the basis for generations of Christmas card messages. Variations of it remain the primary Christmas card greetings, even today. Cole was so pleased with the card that he had two batches of them made to sell, over 2,000 cards in total, for a shilling apiece.

Original specimens of the first Christmas card are now extremely rare and valuable. Only a dozen are known to exist.

First Christmas card printed in 1843 in London

Two of these, including one that has never been used, are part of the Hallmark Historical Collection in Kansas City, Missouri.

By 1860 greeting card firms had been established in Great Britain and in 1896, the London firm of Charles Goodall and Son began printing the first mass-produced Christmas cards.

Victorian Christmas cards tended to be elaborate. The famed English artist Kate Greenaway soon became an established expert in designing cards for Marcus Ward and Co. of London. The cute children from Miss Greenaway's pen were dressed always in high fashion attire and attracted many imitators. Other early Christmas cards carried scenes we might not now consider traditional for the holiday season; instead they featured animals, fairies, and springtime scenes, in celebration of the coming year.

It was not until German lithographer Louis Prang, living in Boston, began producing cards in the 1870s that scenes of the nativity became popular Christmas card motifs. Known now as the "father of the American Christmas card," Prang perfected a lithographic process that enabled as many as 30 colors to be reproduced on one card. He reproduced oil paintings so perfectly that, at times, experts reported, few people could tell his prints from the paintings.

The popularity of his religious cards increased annually, and within a decade (by 1881) Prang was printing five million cards a year, most of them Christmas cards and most of them with a religious theme. Prang's cards became so popular that, it is said, young ladies would mark their social popularity by the "number of Prangs" they received each year.

Turn-of-the-20th-century American cards began to feature more traditional holiday images. Costumed holiday figures graced the fronts of many cards, along with Thomas Nast's cartoons featuring Santa Claus. It was Nast who first drew jolly old St. Nicholas as we picture him today – a fat man with white beard and red suit.

At the turn of the 20th century, German-made Christmas postcards began to flood the world market and this continued until the outbreak of World War I. These penny postcards began to force people like Prang into the background. It was at this time that many of the American card companies were founded, and a return of cards with envelopes was seen.

CHRISTMAS CARDS have long reflected the social norms of an era. As soon as the card industry survived the rigors of the Depression, it came face-to-face with World War II, and with it came flag-carrying Santas and special cards for servicemen.

"Across the Miles" and "Missing You" sentiments reflected the somber reality of the day.

And in 1953, Dwight D. Eisenhower sent the first official White House Christmas card. These cards have traditionally featured images of the White House, decorated for the holiday season.

Christmas cards' appearances have certainly expanded with the technology. While the more traditional cards with holiday symbols – wreaths, bells, candles, religious themes, and Santa Claus – still tend to dominate the market, museum art and even nostalgic Victorian art cards are also still available.

Now, however, it is possible to also send Christmas cards that light up or play tunes like "Frosty the Snowman." Photo companies allow families to produce Christmas cards online, featuring photos of smiling families, children, and even pets, complete with personalized messages. In addition, the resurgence in crafting has led to a return to handmade cards, using techniques from scrap-booking and other paper crafts.

1995 marked the height of the Christmas card industry in the United States, when roughly 2.7 billion cards were sold. Since then, the number of cards sent has steadily declined; by 2011 the number had dropped to 1.5 billion – collateral damage from the digital age. Card companies, such as Hallmark, now allow customers to send e-cards for the holiday season, produced and delivered entirely online.

But in my house, I will not embrace the e-card. I will not send my annual holiday greetings via email or Facebook. I have my own sleigh now, a wooden-and-tin version of the card sleigh from my childhood. And every December I fill it with the cards that arrive: photos of my friends' growing children and messages from my loved ones, reminding me every holiday season how full of peace, love, and joy my life remains.

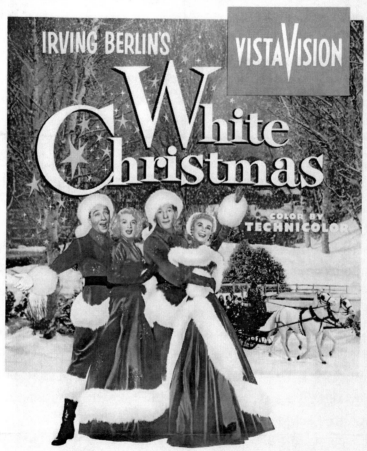

White Christmas

HE DIDN'T THINK IT WAS ANY GOOD. After all, he was a Jewish-American composer, the son of immigrants, whose own holidays as a youth were remembered more for their poverty than for anything else. But he was charged in 1941 with writing songs about every major holiday for a film titled "Holiday Inn," starring Fred Astaire and Bing Crosby.

And Christmas for him was simply a challenge.

His name was Irving Berlin. And he was the most prolific songwriter of American music in the 20th century. Born in 1888, he developed his songwriting talents to produce music still beloved by generations beyond their time. From "Alexander's Ragtime Band" to "There's No Business Like Show Business," Berlin had a talent to not only create a tune that everyone would whistle, but to write lyrics that spoke from the heart of Americans who adored him.

One such example occurred at the end of World War I when Berlin wrote "God Bless America," but decided it did not fit a Broadway revue he was putting together at the time. Instead, he reworked the tune for a Veterans Day program in

1938, when songstress and entertainer Kate Smith introduced it on her radio program. Through the years, the song generated such sentiment that serious efforts were made to replace the national anthem with this patriotic song. Even now, eight decades later during another time of national crisis, that Irving Berlin composition stirs the souls of all Americans.

"I don't think we have any problems with that one, Irving," Bing Crosby said at the first rehearsals, assuring Berlin that "White Christmas" was a winner. He knew then what others would shortly feel as America marched off to World War II: Christmas is full of feeling for home and family and love. And "White Christmas" captured that feeling perfectly:

I'm dreaming of a white Christmas,
Just like the ones I used to know.

These days, we sing "White Christmas" with a Currier and Ives-like scene in mind. But for the folks who heard it for the

Irving Berlin

first time for real, it had a most profound meaning.

The year was 1941. It was a time when folks were possessed with worries of an unstable world, of loved ones being shipped off for war, not knowing when they would be together again and when futures were put on hold. A Christmas "just like the ones I used to know" was definitely something to hope for and a sentiment they shared equally.

For most folks listening on Christmas Day to Bing Crosby's radio show, their thoughts were of separation during Christmases to come. Nobody knew how long the war would last or what the outcome would be. For many, facing Christmas under these circumstances made "White Christmas" a song to listen to with reverence and reflection.

As the war progressed, the song became, in essence, an anthem. Christmas 1943 saw many families torn apart as America fought the war on two fronts. Christmas 1944 was a cold, bitter and frightful time for folks living continents away. This song was cherished on both sides of the ocean, and revered for the sentiment it carried.

By the end of the war, "White Christmas" had become the biggest-selling single of all time. For the next several years it raced up the Top 30 charts no less than 16 times and it remains, to this day, the most popular recorded holiday song of all time.

Where the treetops glisten and children listen
to hear sleigh bells in the snow.

Bing Crosby performed for the troops overseas in countless places during the war. Without fail, he recalls requests for "White Christmas," regardless of the season. "It really got so that I hesitated about doing it because invariably it caused such a nostalgic yearning among the men that it made them sad. Heaven knows that I didn't come that far to make them sad. And for this reason, several times I tried to cut it out of the show. But these guys just hollered for it."

So popular was the recording that Crosby had to re-record it in 1947, because the masters of his 1942 recording session were worn beyond use. The original recording was made on May 29, 1942 for the movie "Holiday Inn." It was recorded with the Ken Darby Singers and the John Scott Trotter Orchestra and the session took just 18 minutes. Crosby starred in the movie with Fred Astaire. After the master recording wore out, Crosby and the John Scott Trotter Orchestra recorded it again on

March 19, 1947.

The original version began with this verse:
"*The sun is shining, the grass is green,*
The orange and palm trees sway.
There's never been such a day
in Beverly Hills, L.A.
But it's December the twenty-fourth,
And I am longing to be up North —"

Crosby's record producer Jack Kapp said the verse was meaningless outside the context of the movie. Therefore, Crosby never used the verse, and the second recording has become the version that became a lasting holiday tradition.

The "Holiday Inn" production showcased a number of Berlin songs, which in themselves became hits, such as "Easter Parade," "Happy Holidays" and "Be Careful ...It's My Heart," but "White Christmas" was to last and last and last. After the movie was released, "White Christmas" won the Academy Award for the best song of 1942.

Well after the close of the war, Crosby starred in a syrupy and plot-challenged holiday film also called "White Christmas" co-starring Danny Kaye, Rosemary Clooney, and Vera Ellen. The movie, released in 1954, was a hit that created another surge in popularity for the song.

The song defined Bing Crosby's career. For over 50 years it has remained the biggest-selling single worldwide with more than 50 million copies, according to *Guinness World Records*. Several other lists cite Elton John's "Candle in the Wind" re-recording in 1997 in memory of Princess Diana as rivaling Crosby's tune for the No. 1 position.

I'm dreaming of a white Christmas
With every Christmas card I write.

"White Christmas" has endured recordings by various artists (there are over 500 versions!) and it has been translated into 25 different languages.

While it is performed each holiday season, it seems to get an unusual amount of attention from the military. Even during the Vietnam War (a war that Crosby privately opposed), "White Christmas" was used as a signal song to waiting Americans who were evacuating the embassy in Saigon in 1975. When the signal phrase "It's 105 degrees and rising" was uttered, followed by the playing of "White Christmas," a mad scramble ensued for waiting helicopters effectively ending America's military presence in Vietnam.

May your days be merry and bright,
and may all your Christmases be white.

There are times when the most impracticable of elements combine to create something special. Such was the case with the creation of "White Christmas." And for most of us today, Christmas is just not Christmas without it.

Bing Crosby and Marjorie Reynolds from the 1942 "Holiday Inn"

DAVID G. STRATMAN

The Christmas Truce

"**S**TILLE NACHT. HEILIGE NACHT.** Alles Schlaft, einsam wacht." The tune was familiar but the lyrics were not.

It was in early morning hours of Christmas Day 1914, only five months into World War I, and German, British, and French soldiers were already sick and tired of the senseless killing. At the end of the carol, a German trooper held Christmas trees lit with pieces of candles up out of the trenches. He yelled "Merry Christmas. You no shoot, we no shoot."

Thousands of troops streamed across a no-man's land strewn with rotting corpses. They sang Christmas carols, exchanged photographs of loved ones back home, shared rations, played football (soccer), kicking around some empty cans, even roasted some pigs. Soldiers embraced men they had been trying to kill a few short hours before.

This Christmas truce spread along the 500-mile Western Front, and soldiers from both sides agreed to warn each other if the top brass forced them to fire their weapons, and to aim high.

Some places along the line renewed the warfare after one day, but at other locations the truce lasted weeks. A shudder

World War I soldiers fraternizing at Christmastime, 1914

ran through the high command on either side. Here was disaster in the making: soldiers declaring their brotherhood with each other and refusing to fight. Generals on both sides declared this spontaneous peacemaking to be treasonous and subject to court-martial.

By March 1915 the fraternization movement had been eradicated and the killing machine put back in full operation. By the time the armistice was signed in November 1918, 15 million men would be slaughtered.

Not many people have heard the story of the Christmas Truce. On Christmas Day 1988, a story in the *Boston Globe* mentioned that a local FM radio host played "Christmas in the Trenches," a ballad about the Christmas Truce – several times – and was startled by the effect. The song became the most requested recording during the holidays in Boston on several FM stations.

"Even more startling than the number of requests I get is the reaction to the ballad afterward by callers who hadn't heard it before," said the radio host. "They telephone me, deeply moved, sometimes in tears, asking, 'What the hell did I just hear?'"

You can probably guess why the callers were in tears. The Christmas Truce story goes against most of what we have been taught about people. It gives us a glimpse of the world as we wish it could be and says, "This really happened once." It reminds us of those thoughts we keep hidden away, out of range of the TV and newspaper stories, that tell us how trivial and mean human life is. It is like hearing that our deepest wishes really are true: the world really could be different.

❋   ❋   ❋

Christmas in The Trenches

THIS SONG IS BASED ON a true story from the front lines of World War I that I've heard many times. [Iain Colquhoun], a Scot, was (a captain and) the commanding officer of the British forces involved in the story. He was subsequently court-martialed for consorting with the enemy and sentenced to death. Only George V spared him from that fate. – John McCutcheon

My name is Francis Toliver, I come from Liverpool.
Two years ago the war was waiting for me after school.
To Belgium and to Flanders, to Germany to here,
I fought for King and country I love dear.

'Twas Christmas in the trenches, where the frost so bitter hung.
The frozen fields of France were still, no Christmas song was sung.
Our families back in England were toasting us that day,
Their brave and glorious lads so far away.

I was lying with my messmate on the cold and rocky ground,
When across the lines of battle came a most peculiar sound.
Says I, "Now listen up, me boys!" each soldier strained to hear,
As one young German voice sang out so clear.

"He's singing bloody well, you know!" my partner says to me.
Soon, one by one, each German voice joined in harmony.
The cannons rested silent, the gas clouds rolled no more,
As Christmas brought us respite from the war.

As soon as they were finished and a reverent pause was spent,
"God Rest Ye Merry, Gentlemen" struck up some lads from Kent.
The next they sang was "Stille Nacht," "'Tis 'Silent Night,'" says I,
And in two tongues one song filled up that sky.

"There's someone coming towards us!" the front line sentry cried.
All sights were fixed on one lone figure trudging from their side.
His truce flag, like a Christmas star, shone on that plain so bright,
As he bravely strode unarmed into the night.

Then, one by one, on either side, walked into No Man's Land,
With neither gun nor bayonet we met there hand to hand.
We shared some secret brandy and wished each other well,
And in a flare-lit soccer game we gave 'em hell.

We traded chocolates, cigarettes, and photographs from home.
These sons and fathers far away from families of their own.
Young Sanders played his squeezebox and they had a violin,
This curious and unlikely band of men.

Soon daylight stole upon us and France was France once more.
With sad farewells we each began to settle back to war.
But the question haunted every heart that lived that wondrous night:
"Whose family have I fixed within my sights?"

'Twas Christmas in the trenches where the frost so bitter hung.
The frozen fields of France were warmed as songs of peace were sung.
For the walls they'd kept between us to exact the work of war
Had been crumbled and were gone forevermore.

My name is Francis Toliver, in Liverpool I dwell,
Each Christmas come since World War I, I've learned its lessons well,
That the ones who call the shots won't be among the dead and lame,
And on each end of the rifle we're the same.

Words and music by John McCutcheon, ©1984

Cover of McCutcheon's sheet music.

EDITOR'S NOTE: Probably the best book on this subject is *Silent Night — The Story of The World War I Christmas Truce* by Stanley Weintraub (New York: The Free Press, 2001). In reality, Captain Colquhoun's court-martial ended in a "reprimand" which was promptly wiped away by General Douglas Hait.

The Christmas Spider

IRGINIA'S CHRISTMAS TRADITIONS are comprised of a variety of customs which came from European sources, primarily in England and Germany. Back when Virginia was being founded, Englishmen came seeking to make money – to find gold or other natural resources. When the first Germans arrived, however, they were chosen to come to the New World for their skills: glassblowing and carpentry.

While these industries were ultimately failures, the German culture succeeded.

It was these early Europeans later in the early eighteenth century who brought the Germanic traditions of Christmas to the New World. To be fair, later most Germans entered Virginia by way of the port city of Philadelphia. They followed the Scots Irish west across Pennsylvania and south into the Great Valley of Virginia. Even though these people were immigrants looking for opportunity, they would never leave behind or forget their legends and folklore.

Probably the most important German tradition was the Christmas tree; today's advent calendars and advent wreaths were Germanic in origin. Candles were burned in German windows to light the way for the Christ Child on Christmas Eve.

Among those stories was a legend, the Christmas Spider. There are several different versions of this wonderful piece of folklore, but what follows is how this Virginia Storyteller tells and re-tells it:

A LONG TIME AGO, in the old country, deep in the mountains where the snow piles high, an industrious woman began her annual Christmas cleaning. She would rise early on the morning of Christmas Eve and set to work. Her family knew to stay out of her way as she cleaned from dawn to dusk. No corner of their modest home was left untouched. Most of the time her husband would take the children out in the morning to chop and stack firewood. In the afternoon they would head far into the forest to search for the perfect Christmas tree. These were important jobs to be sure, but not nearly as important as staying out of mother's way.

Unfortunately, the whispered message to stay out of mother's way was not heard by a family of spiders that had moved inside as fall turned to winter. Suddenly these spiders were fleeing madly for their lives as brooms, brushes, and dust rags came flashing their way. The entire spider family was forced to take refuge in a far corner of the attic, trembling in fear and praying this possessed woman would fall out, exhausted, before reaching the attic. As they clung to one another, each had to feel this was not the Christmas celebration for which they had dreamed and hoped.

Late in the night, sounds of the cleaning frenzy were replaced with the sounds of a family preparing for bed. Soon, all was quiet and the spider family crept from their hiding spot to discover a large, beautifully decorated tree in the center of the house. They raced to the tree, climbed the trunk, sang, danced, and swung from the branches spinning their webs as they celebrated up and down the tree. Finally, when the spider family was so exhausted they could frolic no more, each member of the family found a nook or hollow where the tree's limbs met the trunk – and fell fast asleep.

A few hours before dawn, no one knows how many, the Christmas Visitor arrived in the nice clean home. Different people see the Christmas Visitor differently; for some he is Santa Claus, or Father Christmas, or *Weihnachtsmann* (which translates as the Christmas Man) or for some he is even the Christ Child Himself, come to bless the home. When the Christmas Visitor arrived, he marveled at the tree covered from tip to bottom with gray, sticky webs. The problem was clear and certain.

The Christmas Visitor knew the lady of the house would awake and furiously clear away all the webs and shoo the spiders out of her home. It would destroy their work and leave them homeless on Christmas day. The Christmas Visitor gently reached out and touched the webs. They instantly changed into sparkling, shimmering strands. From that day to this, people remember the two families and the Christmas Visitor by decorating their trees with shiny silver tinsel.

As far as Christmas goes, it does not matter if your ancestors were English, or German, or Early Virginian, or Spider. What matters is that we all celebrate Christ's birth in the most beautiful ways we know.

RUDOLPH
THE RED-NOSED
REINDEER

What About Rudolph?

ROBERT MAY WAS A SHORT MAN, barely five feet in height. He was born in the early part of the last century, that is to say, the 1900s.

Bullied at school, he was ridiculed and humiliated by other children because he was smaller than other boys of the same age. Even as he grew up, he was often mistaken for someone's little brother.

When he left college he became employed as a copywriter with Montgomery Ward, the big Chicago mail order house. He married Evelyn and in due course, his wife presented him with a daughter, Barbara. Then when his little daughter was two years old, tragedy struck; his wife was diagnosed with a debilitating disease. She became bedridden and remained so until she died. Nearly everything he earned went to medication and doctor's bills. Money was short and life was hard.

One evening in early December of 1938 and two years into his wife's illness, four-year-old Barbara climbed onto his knee and asked, "Daddy, why isn't Mummy like everybody else's mummy?" It was a simple question, asked with childlike curiosity. But it struck a personal chord with Robert May.

His mind flashed back to his own childhood. He had often posed a similar question, "Why can't I be tall, like the other kids?" The stigma attached to those who are different is hard to bear. Groping for something to say to give comfort to his daughter, he began to tell her a story. It was about someone else who was different, ridiculed, humiliated, and excluded because of the difference.

Robert told the story in a humorous way, making it up as he went along, in the way that many fathers often do. His daughter laughed, giggled, and clapped her hands as the misfit finally triumphed at the end. She then made him start all over again from the beginning, and every night after that he had to repeat the story before she would go to sleep.

Because he had no money for fancy presents, Robert decided that he would put the story into book form. He had some artistic talent and he created illustrations. This was to be his daughter's Christmas present: The book of the story that she loved so much. He converted the story into a poem.

On the night before Christmas Eve, he was persuaded to attend his office Christmas party. He took the poem along and showed it to a colleague. The colleague was impressed and insisted that Robert read his poem aloud to everyone else at the party. Somewhat embarrassed by the attention, he took the small handwritten volume from his pocket and began to read about the little reindeer with the bright, shiny nose – Rudolph.

At first the noisy group listened in laughter and amusement as the poem unfolded and then his audience became silent and after he finished, they broke into spontaneous applause.

Later, and feeling quite pleased with himself, he went home, wrapped the book in Christmas wrapping and placed it under the modest Christmas tree. To say that his daughter was pleased with her present would be an understatement. She loved it!

When Robert returned to work after the holiday, he was summoned to the office of his head of department. He wanted to talk to Robert about his poem. It seemed that word had got out about his reading at the Christmas party. The head of Marketing was looking for a promotional tool and wondered if Robert would be interested in having his poem published.

Record album for 1961 recording

During the following year, 1939, printed copies of the book were given to every child who visited the department stores of Montgomery Ward, and it eventually became an international bestseller, making Robert a rich man. His wife had unfortunately died during this time, but later he was able to move from the small apartment and buy a big house. He was at last able to provide handsomely for his daughter and a growing family with his second wife.

The story, however, is not quite over.

In 1948, Robert's brother-in-law, songwriter Johnny Marks, used the theme of Robert's poem for a song. Several well-known singers of the day, including Bing Crosby and Dinah Shore, turned down requests to record the tune. Crosby, it is said, declined because he felt is was "too juvenile," admitting later it was a "big mistake."

Marks finally showed the song to a famous film star of the day, Gene Autry, "The Singing Cowboy." Autry, like the others, was inclined to say "no," but his wife talked him into it. It was the "B" side for his record. The rest is history. Autry's 1949 song became a worldwide number one hit, selling 15 million records that year. For many years to come it was the No. 2 best-selling holiday song behind "White Christmas."

There are a variety of back stories about Robert May and Rudolph. In fact, Robert himself gave different versions at several interviews later in his life. Cullen Murphy, writing in 1990 in *The Atlantic* magazine, said the original poem, in contrast to Marks's song, "is full and rich and written in clunky homespun couplets." Rudolph was not one of Santa's deer and did not live at the North Pole in the original poem, but was found by Santa later.

"The fog was worsening on that Christmas Eve," Murphy wrote: "Rudolph is eager to help. Once in harness, Rudolph is no passive point of light. He takes command of Santa's team of proud, mature reindeer he has met for the first time – and skillfully navigates from house to house. As Santa observes publicly upon their return, 'By YOU last night's journey was actually bossed./Without you, I'm certain we'd all have been lost!'"

For reasons unknown, Montgomery Ward never provided a clear story of the beginning of Rudolph. Through the years writers have told the story of Montgomery Ward officials looking for a new Christmas story that could be developed into a promotional book to give away to its holiday customers and, thus, May devised his Rudolph story for the company. Initially it supposedly did not originate to help his daughter cope with her mother's cancer illness; nevertheless, May did give it to his daughter later, the other story goes.

A fantastic Christmas gift came to May years later. Montgomery Ward held the copyright for Rudolph, but May was in severe financial difficulties with medical bills from his wife's long-term illness and pleaded with Sewell Avery, president of Montgomery Ward, to give him the rights to Rudolph. In a gesture of gratitude and understanding Avery conveyed Rudolph and the appropriate rights to May in early January, 1947.

So Rudolph was launched as a nationwide holiday favorite. May wrote two sequels to his original Rudolph: "Rudolph's Second Christmas" (1947) and "Rudolph Shines Again" (1954), published by Maxton Books. Then came a movie short, comic books, children's books published by Golden Books in the late 1950s and finally the 1964 television special that has become a Christmas classic, with Burl Ives as the voice of Sam, the Snowman, telling an expanded version of the Rudolph story.

Little Golden Book, using artwork from 1958

EDITOR'S NOTE: Johnny Marks also wrote several other well-known Christmas tunes including "A Holly Jolly Christmas," recorded in 1963 by Burl Ives, "Rockin' Around the Christmas Tree," first sung by Brenda Lee in 1960, and "Run, Run, Rudolph," popularized by Chuck Berry in 1958. Gene Autry is the only person with five stars on the Hollywood Walk of Fame, awarded for motion pictures, radio, music recording, television, and live theater.

Jingle Bells

"JINGLE BELLS" IS ONE OF OUR FAVORITE Christmas songs and annually is listed as one of the five most-played tunes on the radio throughout the country during the holiday season.

But it was not written for Christmas at all.

It was composed for a Thanksgiving program.

It was first titled "One Horse Open Sleigh."

And that's where the history of "Jingle Bells" gets completely mixed up. There are nearly a half-dozen stories about the origin of the song – when and where. And Massachusetts and Georgia both claim it as their own.

At least three books have been written since 1981 offering completely different versions of its history.

Two things are certain: James Lord Pierpont was the composer, and Oliver Ditson and Co. of Boston published it in August 1857.

Another consensus is that Pierpont wrote the tune for a church Thanksgiving program, reflecting on the approaching winter season. Thus, the original title, "One Horse Open Sleigh." The song was so popular in the church – whatever church it was – that the children decided they want to sing it later the same year in the Christmas season, so a story goes.

But where was it written? Some historians believe it was in Savannah, Georgia, where the composer's brother, the Rev. John Pierpont Jr., was pastor of a Unitarian congregation and James was organist and music director. Others think it was written in Medford, Massachusetts, where their father, the Rev. John Pierpont Sr., was pastor of the First Parish Church.

Hence the reason both states claim ownership.

A Massachusetts plaque in Medford claims that Pierpont composed "Jingle Bells" at Simpson Tavern (since demolished) at 19 High Street in 1850 (not 1856 or 1857 as other traditions believe), having been inspired by the town's popular sleigh races held on nearby Salem Street in the early 1800s. The Tavern was a boarding house with apparently the only piano in town.

In Savannah a historic marker says Pierpont composed the song while employed in the city as music director at his brother's church. He eventually married the daughter of a Savannah mayor, and was finally buried in Savannah's Laurel Grove Cemetery. City historians note that the song was copyrighted and published in 1857 while he was living in Savannah, and was first performed at the church where he worked and his brother preached.

And his words were a reflection of the snows and winter of his youth, even as he dwelt among the live oaks and moss of this very Southern city.

What about the actual jingle bells? A horse-drawn sleigh makes very little noise as it glides across the snow. So leather bands of bells were often attached to the horses. The jingle of the bells, to the canter of the horse or horses, would warn other sleighs that another was approaching.

According to another "Jingle Bell" tradition, Pierpont had the idea for the text of the song when a lady, hearing the tune, said to him: "Mr. Pierpont, what a merry little jingle."

The words of the song also are unusual for a holiday tune – whether Thanksgiving or Christmas. The lyrics talk about fast-gliding sleighs and picking up girls, which may have reflected Pierpont's defiant youthful days when he ran away from his family to go to sea, and later abandoned his first wife for a California gold rush adventure.

Regardless of the meanings or the exact words, the song became extremely popular and was reprinted two years later in 1859 under the title "Jingle Bells, or the One Horse Open Sleigh." Through the years, the song has become the most popular secular song of the Christmas season in the United States and around the world. James Pierpont was inducted into the Song Writers Hall of Fame in 1970.

In 1898, the Edison Male Quartette first recorded the song on an Edison hard wax cylinder as part of a collection of Christmas tunes entitled "Sleigh Ride Party," In 1902, The Haydn Quartet, one of the most popular harmony quartets at the turn of the 20th century, again recorded the tune.

In the 1930s, "Jingle Bells" became an important holiday song in the repertoires of the big bands with Benny Goodman and His Orchestra and Glenn Miller and His Orchestra with Tex Beneke recording the song, in 1935 and 1941, respectively.

It was, however, the recording in 1943 on the Decca label by Bing Crosby and The Andrews Sisters that propelled the song into musical history. It reached No. 19 on the record charts and sold more than a million copies that year. Today, that is still the version most often heard.

Since then, many a major singer has performed and recorded "Jingle Bells." Among those artists are: Frank Sinatra, Luciano Pavarotti, Perry Como, Judy Collins, The Beatles, Duke Ellington, Ella Fitzgerald, Barry Manilow, Nat "King" Cole, and The Million Dollar Quartet (Johnny Cash, Jerry Lee Lewis, Carl

Perkins, and Elvis Presley).

The song has a unique place in musical history. It was the first song broadcast from space. The *Gemini 6* astronauts, Thomas P. Stafford and Walter M. "Wally" Schirra, performed and broadcast the tune on December 16, 1965.

They sent this report to Mission Control in Houston, Texas: "We have an object, looks like a satellite going from north to south, probably in polar orbit.... Looks like it might be going to re-enter soon.... You just might let me pick up that thing....I see a command module and eight smaller modules in front. The pilot of the command module is wearing a red suit...." The astronauts had smuggled a tiny harmonica and sleigh bells onto the spacecraft, and proceeded with their version of "Jingle Bells."

Mission Control suddenly heard the familiar tune with Schirra on the harmonica (Hohner's Little Lady model) and Stafford shaking six miniature bells. Neither sang. Just the tune came over from outer space and those at Mission Control doubled over with laughter. For that day, it certainly was the right stuff.

*   *   *

EDITOR'S NOTE: Medford, Massachusetts is connected with another well-known holiday verse and tune. The poem was written by Lydia Maria Child, a Medford native, and is now the holiday song, "Over the River and Through the Woods." Published in 1844, it, too, was written for Thanksgiving, not Christmas, and was originally entitled, "A Boy's Thanksgiving Day."

Christmas Poems

Christmas Bells (1863)

HENRY WADSWORTH LONGFELLOW

I heard the bells on Christmas Day
Their old, familiar carols play,
And wild and sweet, the words repeat
Of peace on earth, good-will to men!

And thought how, as the day had come,
The belfries of all Christendom
Had rolled along, the unbroken song
Of peace on earth, good-will to men!

'Till ringing, singing on its way,
The world revolved from night to day,
A voice, a chime, a chant sublime
Of peace on earth, good-will to men!

Then from each black, accursed mouth
The cannon thundered in the South,
And with the sound the carols drowned
Of peace on earth, good-will to men!

It was as if an earthquake rent
The hearth-stones of a continent,
And made forlorn the households born
Of peace on earth, good-will to men!

And in despair I bowed my head;
"There is no peace on earth," I said;
"For hate is strong, and mocks the song
Of peace on earth, good-will to men!"

Then pealed the bells more loud and deep:
"God is not dead, nor doth He sleep;
The Wrong shall fail, the Right prevail,
With peace on earth, good-will to men."

❄   ❄   ❄

EDITOR'S NOTE: Longfellow wrote this poem on Christmas Day, 1863 during the American Civil War. Verses four and five in this version reflect the war's despair – including the crippling war wounds of his son Charles. He was also still mourning his beloved wife Fanny, who died in July of 1861. Verse six directly reflects his feelings: "And in despair, I bowed my head; there is no peace on earth, I said." But the end of the poem mirrors his hopes overriding his grief.

Christmas Everywhere (1903)

PHILLIPS BROOKS

Everywhere, everywhere, Christmas tonight!
Christmas in lands of the fir-tree and pine,
Christmas in lands of the palm tree and vine,
Christmas where snow peaks stand solemn and white,
Christmas where cornfields stand sunny and bright;
Everywhere, everywhere, Christmas tonight.

Christmas where children are hopeful and gay,
Christmas where old men are patient and gray,
Christmas where peace, like a dove in his flight,
Broods o'er brave men in the thick of the fight;
Everywhere, everywhere, Christmas tonight.

For the Christ-child who comes is the Master of all,
No place too great and no cottage too small;
The Angels who welcome Him sing from the height,
"In the city of David, a King in His might."
Everywhere, everywhere, Christmas tonight.

Then let every heart keep its Christmas within:
Christ's pity for sorrow, Christ's hatred for sin.
Christ's care for the weakest, Christ's courage for right,
Christ's dread of the darkness, Christ's love for the light.
Everywhere, everywhere, Christmas tonight.

So the stars of the midnight which compass us 'round
Shall see a strange glory, and hear a sweet sound,
And cry, "Look! the earth is aflame with delight,
O sons of the morning, rejoice at the sight!"
Everywhere, everywhere, Christmas tonight!

Christmas Senses (2009)

DEL "ABE" JONES

Christmas trees with twinkling
   lights
Sparkling tinsel spread around
Ornaments and decorations
On the green boughs, hanging
   down.

A wreath of holly on the outside
Mistletoe above the door
Sounds of those Christmas carols
Telling tales of Christmas lore.

Presents wrapped in shiny paper
Tied with pretty ribbons' bows
The wonder in wee ones' eyes
As their anticipation grows.

The chill crispness of the air
Falling crystals of white snow
The family gathered 'round the
   hearth
Warmed by the crackling glow.

Eggnog topped with nutmeg
The pies, candies and cakes
The aroma from the kitchen
Of the oven as it bakes.

A birthday celebration
For that someone up above
Thought and wishes 'round the
   earth
For a world of peace and love.

It's too bad it can't be Christmas
With all its hope and cheer;
It's too bad life can't be lived
Like this day, all through the year.

A Christmas Verse (1765)

ANONYMOUS

When New Year's Day is past and gone;
Christmas is with some people done;
But further some will it extend,
And at Twelfth Day their Christmas end.
Some people stretch it further yet,
at Candlemas they finish it.
The gentry carry it further still
And finish it just when they will;
They drink good wine and eat good cheer
And keep their Christmas all the year.

Ceremony upon Candlemas Eve (c. 1650)

ROBERT HERRICK

Down with the rosemary, and so
Down with the bays and mistletoe;
Down with the holly, ivy, all,
Wherewith ye dress'd the Christmas Hall:
That so the superstitious find
No one least branch there left behind:
For look, how many leaves there be
Neglected, there (maids, trust to me)
So many goblins you shall see.

Poor Robin's Almanac (1715)

ANONYMOUS

Now Christmas comes, 'tis fit that we
Should feast and sing and merry be,
Keep open house, let fiddlers play;
A fig for cold, sing care away!
And may they who thereat repine,
On brown bread and on small beer dine.

Make fires with logs, let the cooks sweat
With boiling and with roasting meat;
Let ovens be heat for fresh supplies
Of puddings, pasties, and minced pies,
And whilst that Christmas doth abide
Let butt'ry-door stand open wide.

Hand up those churls that will not feast
Or with good fellows be a guest,
And hang up those would take away
The observation of that day;
O may they never minced pies eat,
Plum-pudding, roast-beef, nor such meat.

But blest be they, awake and sleep,
Who at that time [a] good house keep
May never want come nigh their door,
Who at that time relieve the poor;
Be plenty always in their house
Of beef, veal, lamb, pork, mutton, souse.

EDITOR'S NOTE: Poor Robin's Almanac first appeared about 1661/1662 and was published in and around London by a variety of printers until 1776. This poem appeared in 1715 and later was reprinted in A Christmas Garland by A. H. Bullen in 1885.

Voices in the Mist (1849)

ALFRED, LORD TENNYSON

The time draws near the birth of
    Christ:
The moon is hid; the night is still;
The Christmas bells from hill to hill
Answer each other in the mist.

Four voices of four hamlets round,
From far and near, on mead and
    moor,
Swell out and fail, as if a door
Were shut between me and the
    sound:

Each voice four changes on the wind,
That now dilate, and now decrease,
Peace and goodwill, goodwill and peace,
Peace and goodwill, to all mankind.

Ceremonies for Christmas (1648)

ROBERT HERRICK

Come, bring with a noise,
My merry, merry boys,
The Christmas log to the firing,
While my good dame, she
Bids ye all be free,
And drink to your heart's desiring.

With the last year's brand
Light the new block, and
For good success in his spending,
On your psalteries play,
That sweet luck may
Come while the log is a-tending.

Drink now the strong beer,
Cut the white loaf here,
The while the meat is a-shredding;
For the rare mince-pie,
And the plums stand by,
To fill the paste that's a kneading.

Acknowledgments

WITHOUT Marshall Rouse McClure's constant and helpful encouragement this volume would never have been completed. Her book design and her successful discovery of countless illustrations have enriched our effort. A hearty thanks to Mary Ann Williamson, my world-class copy editor, who kept commas in the right place and verb tenses consistent.

Earl Hamner's gracious loan of his Christmas story for publication propelled me to collect other stories, and some were written especially for this book by Julie Gochenour, Curtis Badger, Paige Quilter, Anne-Evan Williams, Jeff Westover, Anthony Burcher, Jeanne Nicholson Siler and Bill Tolbert.

A special thanks to other contributors who allowed their work to be reproduced in this volume: Craig Dominey, Dennis Montgomery, Beth Trissel, Ivor Noël Hume, Kristin Alexander, James A. McMahon, David G. Stratman, Leslie Melville and, of course, Earl Hamner.

Sincere appreciation goes to Kristin Terbush Thrower for use of a Santa Claus photograph from her book, *Miller and Rhoads Legendary Santa Claus* (2000, The Dietz Press); Beth Trissel and Julie Gochenour for the images of their family homes; Kristin Alexander for the photograph of her with the Legendary Santa; Eugenia Robinson for the Rockbridge County spiderweb; Paige Quilter for the Richmond nativity scene image; Martha Frances Fortson for the Coleman's Christmas Wonderland photographs; Amy Schindler and Ben Bromley, Earl Gregg Swem Library, College of William and Mary; and Dyron Knick, archivist, Virginia Room, Roanoke Public Libraries.

A very special thanks goes to Del "Abe" Jones for permission to reprint his "Christmas Senses," the lone modern verse selected.

Contributors

KRISTIN ALEXANDER is a native of Richmond, Virginia, and a self-proclaimed "city girl," who now lives a decidedly more rural life with her husband, daughter, and a black cat named "Boo" in West Virginia's eastern panhandle. She actively writes on the Internet and is the author of "What She Said" (www.saidkristin. com), a personal blog that blends family, lifestyle and humor.

CURTIS J. BADGER, a native of Virginia's Eastern Shore, is a freelance author and photographer. Among his books are The Barrier Islands: A Photographic History of Life on Hog, Cobb, Smith, Cedar, Parramore, Metompkin and Assateague; A Naturalist's Guide to the Virginia Coast; and The Wild Coast: Exploring the Natural Attractions of the Mid-Atlantic.

PHILLIPS BROOKS (1835–1893), an Episcopal minister, wrote in 1889 a little-known poem, "Christmas Everywhere" (page 178) during an ocean voyage to Japan. Brooks served briefly as Bishop of Massachusetts and is better known as the author of the Christmas carol "O Little Town of Bethlehem."

ANTHONY BURCHER grew up in Grafton, Virginia and now lives in New Kent County, Virginia. When he is not storytelling throughout the southeast, he works as a camp director, and teaches in Virginia schools for the Jamestown-Yorktown Foundation. He recently published a book, 101 Games That Teach Storytelling Skills.

FRANCIS PHARCELLUS CHURCH (1839–1906), a graduate of Columbia University, had a brief tenure as a war correspondent for The New York Times during the Civil War. Afterward, with his brother, he founded The Army and Navy Journal and Galaxy magazine. When Galaxy merged with The Atlantic Monthly, Church became an editorial writer for The Sun.

CRAIG DOMINEY of Atlanta, Georgia is the founder and producer of The MoonlitRoad.com, a popular Southern Storytelling podcast and website. He is also a freelance writer for numerous publications, and scouts locations for film and television productions.

JULIE ANN GOCHENOUR is a native of the Shenandoah Valley where her forebears were among the first to settle in what became Shenandoah County, Virginia. She holds a master of arts degree in religion (religious communication) from Eastern Mennonite University and a Ph.D. in interdisciplinary studies (communication and religious studies) from Union Institute and University. She teaches communication at James Madison University and lives with her husband, Gary, on his family's working farm just west of Woodstock, Virginia.

EARL HAMNER, now 89, was born in Schuyler, Virginia. A novelist, screenwriter, television writer and producer, he is best known for creating and nurturing CBS television's The Waltons and Falcon Crest. Hamner's novel, Spencer's Mountain, published in 1961, was about his childhood experiences and predated his acclaimed television work. One little-known fact about Hamner is that he was among the cadre of writers who worked with Rod Serling on the award-winning television anthology series, The Twilight Zone (1959-1964).

ROBERT HERRICK (1591–1674) was a 17th-century English poet born in Cheapside, London. He took holy orders in 1623 and became vicar of Dean Prior in Devonshire, but was removed during the English civil war. He returned to Dean Prior in 1662 and remained until his death. He wrote over 2,500 poems, and one of his most well-known poems begins: "Gather ye rosebuds while ye may…"

DEL "ABE" JONES is a native of California who now lives in Florida. Often called "The Poor Man's Poet," this United States Air Force veteran began writing nearly 30 years ago, and his military-related verses are etched on veterans' memorials in Waxahachie, Texas and Loudon, New Hampshire. For a number of years he also worked as a lyricist in Nashville.

MARTIN KOALER is a freelance writer who lives in Tidewater, Virginia and has written for a number of publications, including Southern Living and Country Life, as well as a host of newspapers.

HENRY WADSWORTH LONGFELLOW (1807–1892), a poet and educator, held professorships in modern languages at Bowdoin College, his alma mater, and Harvard College. After his academic career ended in 1854, he wrote full-time and was considered by many to be the most popular American poet of the 19th century. Famed Hollywood songwriter Johnny Marks put Longfellow's poem, "Christmas Bells," to music in 1956 and it was first recorded by Bing Crosby.

JOHN MCCUTCHEON of Charlottesville, Virginia, wrote the ballad in 1984 for his album, Winter Solstice. A storyteller and writer of a number of children's music albums, he is probably best known for his "political and socially conscious songs for adults."

JAMES A. MCMAHON, who prefers to be called "Mac," is a native of Maryland and began his professional career as a professor of economics, but switched to his first love, aviation. Initially he was part of a U. S. government team traveling around the world negotiating aircraft agreements with foreign governments, and he finished his career developing ways to measure the quality of air traffic service provided by the Federal Aviation Administration. He currently flies a 1946 Ercoupe identical to the one Ed Nabb Sr. flew on the first Holly Run to Tangier.

LESLIE MELVILLE, a Scotsman, has been performing professionally as a magician and storyteller for more than 50 years. He currently tours with a storytelling company, "The Tree of Bells Storytellers." This story is used with permission of Leslie Melville at www.thestorytelling-resource-centre.com.

DENNIS MONTGOMERY, a Virginia native, has been editor of Colonial Williamsburg, the Journal of The Colonial Williamsburg Foundation since the spring of 2001, after serving two years as guest editor. From May 1985 to May 1988 he was bureau chief for The Associated Press after a stint with the wire service in Arkansas. He is the author of A Link among the Days: The Life and Times of the Reverend Doctor William Archer Rutherfood Goodwin, and was the recipient of a National Endowment for the Humanities journalism fellowship at the University of Michigan.

IVOR NOËL HUME, a native of England, has lived in Virginia more than 55 years. An internationally known archaeologist, he received an OBE (Officer of the British Empire) from Queen Elizabeth for his contributions to British culture in America. He has been heralded as the "father of historical archaeology," and has discovered and/or excavated more than a score of historic sites. He was longtime director of the Department of Archaeological Research at Colonial Williamsburg. A prolific writer, he has more than 20 major books to his credit.

PAIGE QUILTER, a native of Richmond, Virginia, is a professional business-woman, mother and avid volunteer with deep roots in the Richmond community. In 2002 Norbert Bliley, Richmond Nativity Pageant chairman, approached her to be the next director. Eventually she agreed and served that year as apprentice to director Jeannie Edwards. She has served as director since 2003.

WILLIAM M. E. RACHAL (1910–1980), was editor of publications for the Virginia Historical Society from 1953 until his death, and concurrently in the summer and fall of 1980 served as the society's acting director. This story appeared in Volume 1, Number 3 of the Virginia Cavalcade, the historical magazine published by the Library of Virginia from 1951 until 2002.

PARKE ROUSE JR. (1915–1997) was born in Smithfield, Virginia, and raised in the west end of Newport News. A newspaperman early in his career, he wrote many well-loved books and articles during his work as director of Jamestown Festival Park and the Yorktown Victory Center, and later into his retirement years as regular contributor to the Daily Press newspaper. This Christmas story gives a wonderful view of Southside Virginia, south of the James River. Similar vignettes can be found in his book, Below the James Lies Dixie, published in 1968 by The Dietz Press.

JEANNE NICHOLSON SILER, despite being born in Ohio and starting school in Hawaii, has lived in Virginia longer than anywhere else — so far. She began a career in journalism in Williamsburg as a student correspondent in the Richmond Times-Dispatch news bureau, and has since written about tugboat races in Puget Sound, attended a press conference with Captain Kangaroo, and compiled an African American community history for Martinsville, Virginia. A gold-painted star with a macaroni border decorates the top of her Christmas tree each December.

DR. DAVID G. STRATMAN wrote a version of this story in his book, We CAN Change the World: The Real Meaning of Everyday Life, published in 1991 by New Democracy Books. Stratman is co-author of "Thinking about Revolution," (2011) which can be found at newdemocracyworld.org.

ALFRED, LORD TENNYSON (1809–1892), 1st Baron Tennyson, was Poet Laureate of Great Britain from 1850 until his death in 1892, during Queen Victoria's reign. His selection (page 180) was originally canto 104 in his lengthy poem, "In Memoriam A. H. H." written between 1833 and 1849 as a tribute to his friend, Arthur Henry Hallam, and an attempt to cope with Hallam's death.

BETH TRISSEL, a native Virginian, lives on a Shenandoah Valley farm with her husband, her high school sweetheart. This story is from Shenandoah Watercolors, her memoir about gardening and country life. She is also an award-winning, multi-published historical romance author with The Wild Rose Press. More information is available at Bethtrissel.wordpress.com.

BILL TOLBERT has been a journalist for almost 40 years, working for newspapers in his native West Virginia and his adopted Virginia, holding a variety of writing and editing positions. Along the way he has received more than a dozen state press association awards for his writing. In addition, he is a member of the editorial staff of the Virginia State Golf Association and a frequent writer for Virginia Golfer magazine, the association's publication. Currently he is a local news editor with The Free Lance-Star in Fredericksburg.

BOOKER T. WASHINGTON (1856–1915) wrote this story in 1907 about his early Christmas memories in Franklin County, Virginia, prior to the Civil War. It was prepared for publication in Southern Life and Tuskegee Student magazines. The first principal of Tuskegee Institute (now Tuskegee University), Washington was educated at Hampton Institute (now Hampton University). In 1901 his autobiography Up From Slavery gained national attention detailing his life from "slave to school master." The Booker T. Washington National Monument near Hardy in Franklin County, Virginia, is operated by the National Park Service and is the site of Washington's birthplace — a former tobacco farm.

JEFF WESTOVER of Richmond, Utah is the founder of My Merry Christmas. com, the world's largest year 'round Christmas community and the Internet's longest ongoing celebration of Christmas, making merry online since 1991. He is the CEO of Merry Network LLC, a family of Christmas-oriented web sites anchored by a year 'round Christmas radio station, Merry Christmas Radio.

ANNE-EVAN WILLIAMS is a native Virginian and has been a professional educator for more than a dozen years. She enjoys writing whenever she gets the opportunity. Currently, she is headmistress at Ridgewood School in Springfield, Ohio, the oldest independent private school in that state.

Illustration Notes

Page 8 — The steamboat Smithfield worked the Chesapeake Bay and James River for many years, often making the run from Norfolk to Richmond. 1934 was the last year of service for the steamboat.   Page 16 — This illustration was adapted from Frank Leslie's Illustrated Newspaper, December 26, 1857, entitled "Winter Holydays in the Southern States — Plantation Frolic on Christmas Eve."   Page 20 — Taken from part of the original Frank Leslie's Illustrated drawing. See page 16.   Page 29 — The Santa Claus Special rolls into Kingsport, Tennessee, circa 1983. From the archives of the City of Kingsport.   Page 30 — This image was adapted from "Washington Crossing the Delaware" by Emanuel Gottlieb Leutze. The original was destroyed during World War II in Germany and the second version is in the Metropolitan Museum of Art in New York City.   Page 38 — Author Beth Churchman Trissel with her brother John celebrate a wintry holiday at the Churchman family home.   Page 44 — This detail of Chief Powhatan (top) and Captain John Smith (lower in circle below the fire) was taken from an engraving in Smith's Generall Historie of 1623.   Page 47 — Engraving of Captain John Smith was taken from his map of New England in 1614.   Page 50 — "Father and Son Picking Christmas Tree" by German painter Franz Krüger. Page 58 — This Civil War-era photograph depicts cooking in a Confederate camp and most probably was taken in North Carolina. A pot (center) hangs from a stick frame.   Page 64 — Engraving was drawn by Richmond, Virginia-born watercolorist, illustrator and painter William Ludwell Sheppard about 1900. It depicts the "Angel of Marye's Heights," Richard Kirkland.   Page 66 — Richard R. Kirkland's portrait apparently was made early in the Civil War. This image supplied by the Camden, S. C. Archives   Page 67 — Battlefield photographer Violet Clark of Tennessee created this image of the "Angel of Marye's Heights" monument on the Fredericksburg battlefield by well-known sculptor Felix de Weldon. The memorial was dedicated on September 29, 1965. De Weldon's most recognized work is the Marine Corps War Memorial depicting the raising of the flag on Iwo Jima during World War II.
Page 70 — The Eastern Red Cedar is the Eastern Shore's homegrown Christmas tree.   Page 76 — A meal is prepared in an 18th-century plantation kitchen.
Page 79 — Adapted from a colonial church scene painted by Wordsworth Thompson, now part of the Metropolitan Museum of Art Collection.   Page 84 — Author Kristin Alexander sits on the lap of "Legendary Santa" in 1975.   Page

89 – The cover photograph for "Miller & Rhodes – Legendary Santa Claus" by Kristin Terbush Thrower is used by author's permission. Page 96 – Mary, Joseph, the baby Jesus and little angels from the Richmond Nativity Pageant, circa 1993. Page 102 – Yule Log Bearers enter the Great Hall of the Sir Christopher Wren Building at the College of William and Mary, circa 1936. Courtesy of the Special Collections Research Center, Earl Gregg Swem Library, College of William and Mary. Page 108 – "Night Scene of the Electric Star on Mill Mountain" is a post card published in 1950 by the Asheville Post Card Co., Asheville, North Carolina. Page 112 – Photograph is courtesy of Bob Kinsey, one of the original Mill Mountain Star builders. Page 114 – Courtesy of the Virginia Room, Davis Collection, Roanoke Public Library. Page 116 – Entitled "Christmas in the South – Egg Nog Party," this engraving was drawn by William Ludwell Sheppard and appeared in Harper's Weekly, Dec. 31, 1870. Page 121 – "Christmas in the Country" is by Inigo Barlow after a painting by Samuel Collings, circa 1791. Page 122 – Children view a Santa from the Coleman Collection at the Portsmouth Art & Cultural Center. Courtesy of Portsmouth Museums Foundation. Page 127 – Coleman Collection comes alive in a holiday tableau. Courtesy of Portsmouth Museums Foundation. Page 128 – Santa Claus now accompanies the annual Holly Run to Tangier Island in 2011. Washington Post photo is by Sarah L. Voisin. Page 130 – Photograph by Joe Della Barba, 2009, Courtesy of tangierhollyrun.com Page 130 – Photograph by Karen Helfert, 2010, courtesy of the Southside Sentinel, Urbanna, Virginia. Page 136 – Virginia O'Hanlon on her new bicycle, circa 1895. Page 140 – The "Peace on Earth, Good Will Toward Men" card was designed by Frederick Dielman and won third prize in 1882 in the Prang Popular Prize card contest. Page 146 – Paramount Pictures had this poster designed for the movie, "White Christmas," when the film was released in 1954; it was meant for theatrical display. Originals of this poster now sell for about $2,500. Page 151 – Bing Crosby and Marjorie Reynolds sing a duet of "White Christmas" in the 1942 movie, "Holiday Inn." Martha Mears dubbed Reynolds' voice. Page 152 – English and German troops play "football" (soccer) in no-man's-land on Christmas Day 1914 just outside of Armentieres in northern France. Page 154 – German soldiers of the 134th Saxon Regiment are photographed with men of the Royal Dublin Fusiliers near St. Yvon, north of Ploegsteert Woods in the Ypres Salient. Photograph is by 2nd Lt. Cyril Drummond, 135th Battery, Royal Field Artillery. Drummond said the troops came out and exchanged cigars and tobacco and "I lined them all up and took a photograph." Page 160 – A spider web was captured by Rockbridge County photographer Eugenia Robinson. Page 162 – Montgomery Ward printed this book as a Christmas promotion, circa 1939. Page 167 – An early Little Golden Book version of "Rudolph, the Red-nosed Reindeer." Page 170 – Jingle bells encircle this horse in a vintage photograph.

About the Editor

WILFORD KALE, a longtime resident of Williamsburg, Virginia, is retired from the *Richmond Times-Dispatch* and the Virginia Marine Resources Commission, a state agency. In the past decade he has written and/or edited nine books, including compiling and editing books on the history of the Jamestown Settlement of 1607 and Hampton, Virginia. (The original material in both volumes was authored by Parke Rouse Jr.) He also wrote *Hark Upon the Gale, An Illustrated History of the College of William and Mary in Virginia*. His new volume of presidential biographies and election results will be published in early 2013. In his spare time, he has served on the James City County Planning Commission and in 2012 served an interim term as Jamestown District representative on the James City County Board of Supervisors.

During the Christmas holidays in Williamsburg, Mr. Kale has played Santa Claus at Christmas Town at Busch Gardens, and at Yankee Candle.

About the Designer

MARSHALL ROUSE MCCLURE, a native Virginian, was reared in Williamsburg, graduated from St. Catherine's School in Richmond, attended Hollins College in Roanoke and received a

bachelor of fine arts degree from Old Dominion University. Always interested in the arts, she became involved with designing books for the Donning Co. Publishers in Virginia Beach and later branched out into freelance designing and editing – everything from scientific journals to wartime memoirs. Her father was Parke Rouse Jr., noted Virginia author and historian, and after his death in 1997, McClure began to work with some of his published and unpublished materials. She designed two books of his writings, "Jamestown's Story: Act One of the American Dream" (2005), and "Hampton in the Bygone Days" (2010).

She is founder and owner of Parke Press in Norfolk, which has published a number of volumes including "After the Gunboats Landed: A Memoir by George Ben West," edited by Parke Rouse Jr.; "Letters to Shirley: A World War I Aviator's Letters Home;" "Summer People: How Nudists, Boozers and One Headless Turkey Influenced a Boy's Life;" and "Along Hampton's Waterfront: A Historic Tour in Vintage Postcards."

CPSIA information can be obtained at www.ICGtesting.com
Printed in the USA
LVOW06*0449161013

357044LV00002BA/2/P

9 780988 396906